WORLD WAR II
CINCINNATI

ROBERT EARNEST MILLER

WORLD WAR II
CINCINNATI

FROM THE FRONT LINES
TO THE HOME FRONT

THE
History
PRESS

Published by The History Press
Charleston, SC 29403
www.historypress.net

Front cover, top left: Courtesy of Xavier University Archives.

First published 2014

Manufactured in the United States

ISBN 978.1.62619.455.7

Library of Congress CIP data applied for.

This book is dedicated to Dr. Roger Daniels, a prolific scholar, generous mentor, friend and the person who is most responsible for cultivating my interest in this topic.

CONTENTS

CINCINNATI AND WAR

Four days after Imperial Japan attacked U.S. forces at Pearl Harbor, Nazi Germany declared war on the United States. Within a matter of days, public opinion, which had been sharply divided over the fighting in Europe, now stood firm. *Cincinnati Post* columnist Alfred Segal summarized the city's reaction to the swiftly changing international crisis in this way: "There was no longer any isolationism. We had all been brought together under the butcher knife." The nation's entry into World War II ushered in a new era of American history. Over the short run, fifteen million men and women served in the armed forces. Countless others donned factory overalls to fuel the effort of the "arsenal of democracy." Still others gave willingly of their time and energy on the home front to support the war effort. Everyone had a part to play. After the war, victory over the Axis powers produced equally dramatic results in the United States. Women who joined in the war effort remained in the paid labor force, returning veterans crammed onto college campuses, larger families and suburban homes became more prevalent and a new postwar foe, the Soviet Union, challenged the United States for global dominance. The same forces that transformed our nation during the war years also altered the political, social, economic and cultural landscape of Cincinnati.

At the time of America's entry into World War II, it was safe to say that the city of Cincinnati had been no stranger to the periodic demands and intrusions of war. Two years after the city's founding, in 1790, President George Washington established a frontier outpost on the banks of the Ohio River, just opposite the mouth of the Licking River, in the Old Northwest

Territory. Fort Washington served as an important military garrison from which the president launched three separate military expeditions into northwestern Ohio to deal with the threat posed by Little Turtle, the war chief of the Miami people. After the Treaty of Grenville was signed in 1795, which mitigated the danger of subsequent Native American attacks, the fort fell into disuse. In 1803, the Newport Barracks replaced Fort Washington as a regional outpost for the military. Nine years later, when the young Republic went to war with Great Britain for a second time, Cincinnati again served as a staging ground for military conflicts farther north, on American and Canadian soil.

As Cincinnati developed into a teeming river city in the 1840s, it lost many of its frontier characteristics. Indian wars gave way to conflicts in faraway locales that were designed to expand the geographical footprint of the United States and fulfill its sense of Manifest Destiny. In 1846, Camp Washington, situated just north of downtown Cincinnati, served as a training camp and point of departure for more than five thousand troops headed to fight in the Mexican War.

War seemed much more immediate and sobering to Cincinnatians after Confederate guns fired on Fort Sumter, embroiling the nation in four long years of bloody fighting. While Cincinnati stood on the periphery of most of the violence and battles fought during the American Civil War, its residents were subjected to unparalleled demands and sacrifices. Recruits trained at nearby Camp Dennison, sixteen miles northeast of the city on the banks of the Little Miami River. Men were drafted and compelled to serve in the military. The home front contended with its own set of shortages and privations, and morale sagged as the war continued.

Owing to the war's length and intensity, public support for war aims was always in flux. Support for the Union cause remained fractured, at best. Abolitionists, such as Levi Coffin and John Rankin, who championed the rights of oppressed slaves before the war, hoped the conflict would be used to eradicate slavery once and for all. Others rallied around the cause of the Union and Federal supremacy. On the other hand, a sizeable number of Cincinnatians sympathized, openly and unashamedly, with the Confederate cause.

Twice during the years of conflict, the war elbowed its way into the everyday lives of Cincinnatians. In 1862, during a brief period of imposed martial law, General Lew Wallace, who was in charge of Union forces protecting the city, ordered the construction of a pontoon bridge to span the Ohio River. In five short days, the task was complete, and some seventy thousand troops and civilian volunteers crossed the river and erected a line of rifle pits and earthen-work fortifications in the foothills of northern Kentucky. The anticipated Confederate attack never came. Cincinnatians were not so lucky the following year. In mid-July 1863, John Hunt Morgan—a thirty-eight-year-old Kentucky hemp manufacturer turned cavalryman—led a daring two-week assault across southeastern Indiana and a large swath of southern Ohio, including Cincinnati. The timing of the attack, just days after Robert E. Lee's unsuccessful offensive in Gettysburg, might have led Cincinnatians to overestimate the capabilities of the Confederacy to launch a series of such attacks. As it turned out, Morgan's men inflicted little real or lasting damage before they were captured in Salineville, near the Ohio-Pennsylvania border. While Morgan's Raid set tongues wagging and led to tall tales about run-ins with Rebel vagabonds, the Civil War, like no other war before it, left real and lasting scars on the people of Cincinnati for several generations.

Near the dawn of the twentieth century, the United States had defeated the last of the remaining Native Americans. The West, in the eyes of the federal government, had been tamed. The country set its sights on new frontiers. The Spanish-American War, which began in 1898, led Cincinnatians to fight in the Caribbean in defense of Cuban independence and in the Pacific against Filipino insurgents. The city's biggest connection to that war came

The 6th Regiment, "Heroes of San Juan Hill", before leaving Ft. Thomas, Ky., 1898.

During the Spanish-American War, volunteers from Ohio, Indiana and Kentucky joined to form the U.S. Army Sixth Infantry Regiment. These soldiers departed from Newport and eventually participated in combat in Cuba with Teddy Roosevelt and his Rough Riders. *Courtesy of Public Library of Cincinnati and Hamilton County.*

when President William McKinley tapped an ambitious young Cincinnati lawyer, William Howard Taft, to serve as the governor general of the Philippines. Taft transplanted his family to the islands, where he worked for several years. He implemented several far-reaching reforms in civilian government and infrastructure that helped prepare the newly acquired territory for independence.

Young men again responded to the call of duty in 1917 to fight in the trenches in France and Belgium after the United States entered World War I. Men were drafted to serve in the armed forces, but before many of them completed their basic training, an armistice was declared. Returning troops passed under a victory arch erected near the intersection of Fifth and Main Streets in downtown Cincinnati. Etched on the arch was this simple inscription: "Honor for Duty Nobly Done."

For a generation that had welcomed the notion that the Great War would be, in author H.G. Wells's words, "a war to end all wars," it was especially disheartening to watch Europe and Asia tilt toward military aggression and war in the 1930s. World War II, the second such global conflict in the course of one generation, was like no other war. Everyone was affected by the demands of war, as vast armies of combatants as well as noncombatants joined in the war effort. British prime minister Winston Churchill referred to the Second World War as "a people's war." Even before the United States became a full-fledged belligerent, President Franklin D. Roosevelt urged Americans to think of the conflict as "a total war." For the most part, those Americans who lived through this dynamic era—rich or poor, young or old, male or female—believed that America was waging "total war," and they responded to the demands of their government. Few aspects of daily life remained untouched by the conflict.

World War II holds a special place of interest for me. It is distant enough as a historical event to allow me a measure of objectivity. It is close enough for me to appreciate its reverberations on the world we live in. This book is a reflection of my long-standing and enduring interest in the impact of war on American culture. As a student of American history, I performed research on federal efforts to enact civilian defense and morale programs for the home front. After completing my dissertation, I had the opportunity to work as a project historian on the now permanent exhibit at the Cincinnati Museum Center entitled "Cincinnati Goes to War: A Community Responds to Total War." I followed up that work with a short, illustrated history of Cincinnati's home front experiences in *Cincinnati: The World War II Years* (2004). Both of those projects convinced me that Cincinnati's experience during these challenging times reflected broader national trends.

With each day, the World War II generation grows smaller. As we approach the seventy-fifth anniversary of American entry into the war, some memories have faded. Many of the nuances and challenges of this era have been forgotten or overgeneralized. It has become commonplace to think of America's involvement in this conflict as a "good war." Likewise, those people who lived through the event are often shrouded in the mantle of "the greatest generation," whether they asked for such recognition or not. This book takes a slightly different tack. America's version of "total war," we will find, created as many opportunities for bravery, self-sacrifice and heroism as it did for fear, self-doubt and disagreements. This book, in its own way, will attempt to show how Cincinnatians, well-known individuals as well as common folk, responded to the demands of World War II in ordinary as well as extraordinary ways. During the time spent writing and researching this book, I was either reminded or discovered anew just how important a role Cincinnati and its citizens played in furthering the war effort.

One of the real joys in writing this book involved the wonderful response I received from local archives, libraries and historical societies throughout the city. Tim McCabe, the archivist at Xavier University, provided me with access to images and textual materials about his university's role in the war. His counterpart at the University of Cincinnati, Kevin Grace, extended faculty privileges to visit our school's archive several times. Kevin Proffitt, the senior archivist at the Jacob Rader Marcus Center of the American Jewish Archives and a former colleague, welcomed me back to his top-flight repository. Richard Hamilton allowed me access to little-used parish histories at the Archives of the Archdiocese of Cincinnati. Dennis Harrell, the archivist at Christ Church Cathedral of Cincinnati, and Lindsay McLean, archivist at the Indian Hill Historical Society, were also generous with their collections. Chris Smith opened my eyes to the Greater Cincinnati Memory Project at the Public Library of Cincinnati and Hamilton County. Megan Berneking fielded many queries about Eugene Goosens and the Cincinnati Symphony Orchestra. Ruthann Spears, of the Cincinnati Parks Board, also offered assistance. Great Parks of Hamilton County gave me permission to include two rare images from the 1930s that appeared in a park history book I had written several years ago. Chris Eckes, the curator for the Cincinnati Reds Hall of Fame, and Greg Rhodes, the team's historian, both offered valuable advice and guidance about the history of baseball in the war years as well as the history of the franchise during the conceptual stages of this project. Sue Coppin, of the University of Adelaide in Australia, provided me with the image of Eugene Goosens after a last-minute request.

This book benefited from the careful and thorough editing skills of my good friend Dr. Terri Premo, formerly of the University of Cincinnati. Her thoughtful comments and criticisms improved the book immeasurably. Greg Dumais at The History Press helped shepherd this book at every stage of its development.

The final, and surely most important, recognition goes to my family: my wife, Therese, and daughter, Emma. They were true home front heroes in the ways they supported me for the "duration" of this labor of love. Happily, we kept home front casualties to a minimum.

Chapter 1

PAROCHIAL METROPOLIS

A City Touched by War, 1940

Since the early 1930s, world peace and economic stability had been threatened by the rise of strong, militaristic governments. Japan invaded Manchuria in 1931 and mainland China in 1937. In Europe, Fascist Italy launched a military expedition in Ethiopia in 1935 while Adolf Hitler carefully and purposefully rebuilt Nazi Germany by annexing Austria and seizing portions of the Czech Republic. Only after Nazi Germany launched an attack on Poland on September 1, 1939, did Great Britain and France stand firm against any further acts of aggression. Both countries declared war on Hitler's Germany. For the second time in less than twenty years, the world had been thrust into the clutches of global warfare.

All watched in horror in the next few weeks as Nazi Germany and the Soviet Red Army partitioned Poland. Officially, the United States expressed a desire to remain neutral. Congress had crafted a series of neutrality acts in the 1930s that were shaped and informed by the events of 1917. These laws put strict limits on American passengers' ability to travel into war zones, placed tight restrictions on any lines of credit to countries at war and kept U.S. manufactures from trading with belligerent countries. All of this was done with the clear and express purpose of keeping America out of Europe's wars.

National public opinion polls in the United States focused mostly on the situation in Europe. Respondents consistently voiced a preference for a British and French victory. Moreover, Americans felt that it was acceptable to relax the "cash and carry" restriction of the neutrality laws to enable the United States to provide more material aid. The editors of the *News Record*, the student newspaper of the University of Cincinnati, echoed that sentiment in October 1940. Speaking on behalf of its male students—who would be most directly affected if the United States got involved in the war—the editors asserted: "College students do not want to take part in a European conflict, but if the United States is threatened, they will bear arms."

Humanitarian relief groups began to spring up in Cincinnati as more and more of Europe and Asia were overrun in brutal fashion and occupied by military aggressors. Cincinnatians raised funds for Chinese as well as European victims. Interestingly, some Queen City residents reserved their greatest outrage and harshest judgments for Joseph Stalin and Communist Russia instead of Adolf Hitler and the Nazis. When Soviet forces invaded Finland in December 1939, Harold Ihlendorf, a local funeral home director, expressed to an *Enquirer* reporter his deep sympathy for the Finnish people, "whose country is being invaded by the most tyrannical nation in the world."

During the first several months of the conflict, aside from the occasional humanitarian impulse, most Cincinnatians regarded the fighting in Europe and Asia as faraway, distant conflicts. Residents of the Queen City, like most Americans, had just started to experience a measure of economic stability after enduring eleven years of the worst and longest depression in American history. As regrettable as the actions of Nazi Germany, Stalinist Russia and Imperial Japan might have been, matters of the pocketbook tended to weigh more heavily on the minds of Cincinnatians. The situation in Europe would have to grow more dire before Cincinnatians felt like stakeholders in the conflict. Ultimately, it would take a surprise attack on American soil by Germany's ally Imperial Japan to jar America out of its complacency.

In order to understand and appreciate the full impact that the U.S. entry into the war had on the nation—and more specifically, on the people of Cincinnati—it would be wise to survey briefly what the city looked like in 1940, a little more than twenty-three months before the fateful attack on Pearl Harbor. How recognizable were the city's dated features, institutions and landmarks to our eyes?

The earlier generations of immigrants who had decided to make Cincinnati their home had come from a wide range of areas. Like many frontier cities, Cincinnati offered promise and hope. For those new arrivals to the Queen City who came from larger cities, around 1940, Cincinnati likely seemed quaint and parochial. In the eyes of individuals who migrated from more rural environs, Cincinnati offered most of the trappings of a teeming metropolis. Between those varying perspectives lay some version of the truth. Cincinnatians surely enjoyed a small-town feel—a city suspicious of strangers and mired in its sense of traditions—and was generally comfortable with itself. Sunday drives, church festivals and cold bottles of beer at the ballpark best reflected Cincinnati's small-town charms to some residents. At the same time, by 1940, it seemed very much like a city on the upswing, confident about its future. Bustling industries, efficient government and a thriving cultural landscape painted a different image for others.

First and foremost, Cincinnati was a river city. The Ohio River defined much of its early history and economic vitality. Water continued to play an important role into the 1820s, when city and state officials began construction on the Miami and Erie Canal, which eventually linked Toledo (on the banks of Lake Erie) to Cincinnati (on the Ohio River). The path of the canal flowed through the low-lying terrain of the Mill Creek Valley, situated just to the west and north of the city. When the canal was finally disbanded in the early twentieth century, Canal Street, which separated the predominantly German neighborhood of Over the Rhine from the central business district, was renamed Central Parkway and converted into an attractive boulevard, complete with new stores, such as the Alms and Doepke Building.

As its population base grew and its industrial base expanded in the early twentieth century, so did Cincinnati's footprint, largely through annexation efforts. The downtown area, which contained numerous stores for retail,

The Miami and Erie Canal opened for business in 1845. It served Cincinnati businesses for decades before finally closing in the early 1900s. In the 1940s, the same canal bed between Cincinnati and Lockland was used for a more modern highway. *Courtesy of Public Library of Cincinnati and Hamilton County.*

50 : – CENTRAL PARKWAY, CINCINNATI, OHIO.

Central Parkway, once the final leg of the Miami and Erie Canal, became a vibrant area of business for Cincinnati. *Courtesy of Public Library of Cincinnati and Hamilton County.*

entertainment, food, banking and other sundry purposes, was relatively compact. The Mill Creek Valley to the west of the city ran north to south, from Lockland and Ivorydale (the home of Proctor & Gamble) and from Camp Washington and Brighton-Mowhawk down to the West End. In 1932, Mayor Russell Wilson dedicated the Western Hills Viaduct, a two-tier Art Deco bridge that connected downtown Cincinnati to the western suburbs of Cheviot, Westwood and Fairmount, neighborhoods that had been relatively isolated from city life. Another corridor of communities lay to the north and east of the city. Such neighborhoods as Avondale, Evanston, Norwood, Oakley, Madeira and Indian Hill, each with its distinct identity, rounded out the "seven hills of Cincinnati." By the late 1920s, city leaders, after many years of cost overruns, finally quit construction on a subway system that would have linked the downtown region to outlying neighborhoods as far north as Norwood. At about the same time that the city turned its back on one form of mass transit, it warmly embraced the even newer technology of commercial aviation. Lunken Airport, located just east of the city, became a busy hub of activity for Embree Air in 1927. Two smaller airfields in Blue Ash and Sharonville accommodated additional air traffic. By 1940, a labyrinth of state and county roads, buses and streetcars linked the various outlying communities with downtown Cincinnati.

Even when the country lapsed into the Great Depression, Cincinnati seemed at least partially immune to some of the miseries that befell much of the nation. Massive construction projects kept on schedule, even during the depths of the Depression. In 1931, builders completed work on Union Terminal, which consolidated several competing rail lines under one roof. That same year, Carew Tower, the city's tallest and most elegant skyscraper, opened its doors to tenants and customers.

The U.S. economy hit rock bottom in 1933. Unemployment levels soared to unprecedented heights. On average, one out of four Americans had lost his or her job. President Franklin D. Roosevelt and his Democrat-controlled Congress ushered in "an alphabet soup" of federal agencies and programs designed to turn around the sagging economy. Federal dollars trickled into Cincinnati and put people to work on a variety of projects. Despite the fact that residents of Cincinnati and Hamilton County were represented by Republicans in Congress, the Queen City's workers benefited from New Deal programs that put people back to work. The federal government spent roughly $1 million on construction projects that benefited Cincinnati and Hamilton County during the Depression decade. In 1935, Works Progress Administration (WPA) workers doubled the size of Nippert Stadium on the campus of the University of Cincinnati. WPA crews worked for nearly two years grading, draining and landscaping public golf courses at Sharon Woods in Sharonville and California near the banks of the Ohio River, just east of the city. Civilian Conservation Corps (CCC) crews beautified nearby Mount Airy Forest, planting trees and building hiking trails for future generations to enjoy.

In addition to the economic challenges posed by job shortages, Cincinnatians faced other types of adversity. When families struggled to put food on the table during the lean years of the Depression, city officials responded by converting vacant lots into community gardens. In January 1937, Cincinnati residents also had to deal with a flood of biblical proportions when the banks of the Ohio River crested at 79.9 feet. The flood was one of the worst natural disasters in the history of the state. It shut down portions of the city for ten days, disrupting normal patterns of activity. Typically, the flood brought out the best in people. Stricken families were rescued from rooftops. Volunteers made sure that food and water made its way to needy individuals and families. Throughout the crisis, Cincinnatians demonstrated a sense of community spirit, generosity and compassion. This resiliency would serve its citizenry well during the years of crisis in the 1940s.

During the Great Depression, Works Progress Administration crews built dams; constructed roads, bridges and trails; and built an eighteen-hole public golf course at Sharon Woods. *Courtesy of Great Parks of Hamilton County.*

After eleven long years of economic depression, Cincinnati boasted a vibrant and revived city center, with a diversified base of industry, commerce and agriculture. The business community was cautiously optimistic. Cincinnati Milling Machine laid claim to being the largest global manufacturer of machine tools. The city had also become a leading manufacturer in soaps as well as playing cards. The expansion of the city's population in 1940 to more than 456,000 made Cincinnati the seventeenth-largest city in the country. Over the decades of the nineteenth century, large numbers of Germans and Irish had helped shape the city's ethnic identity. Just before the onset of the Great War, sizeable numbers of African American migrants from the rural South traveled north, adding to the city's diverse population. By 1940, African Americans represented about 10 percent of the city's population.

Culturally, Cincinnati had much to offer. Townsfolk kept abreast of current events through three daily newspapers. The Republican-leaning *Cincinnati Enquirer*, the oldest of the three, had taken on the chore of serving as the city's morning paper since the 1880s. Two afternoon papers, the *Cincinnati Times-Star* and the *Cincinnati Post*, offered more independent and Democratic-friendly views, respectively. Three important weekly newspapers—the *Free Press* (a German-language paper), the *Catholic Telegraph* (the official organ of the Archdiocese of Cincinnati) and the *American Israelite* (first published by Rabbi Isaac M. Wise in 1854)—reached smaller audiences.

Radio was still relatively new in 1940. Listeners could tune in to programming on five different radio stations on the AM dial. Programming was rudimentary by current standards. In many cases, stations were only on the airwaves during daytime hours. WLW was the exception in every sense of the word. In 1922, Powell Crosley Jr., a Cincinnati radio manufacturer, received permission from the Federal Communications Commission to purchase the commercial license for WLW. For several years in the Depression decade, the 500,000-watt station was one of the country's largest radio stations and could transmit its signal from a tower about twenty-five miles to the north in Mason, Ohio, to such faraway locations as Latin America. In the 1930s, WLW was considered a rival to NBC; it recruited its own writers and performers and produced its own shows.

The emergence of commercial radio in the 1920s also helped build fan interest in a variety of professional- and collegiate-level sports. In 1934, Crosley purchased the Cincinnati Reds, the oldest franchise in professional baseball. One year later, with the help of general manager Lee McPhail, the Reds hosted the first big-league night game at Crosley Field, located on Western Avenue in the West End. The event attracted national publicity when President Roosevelt symbolically flicked on the switch from the White House to illuminate the festivities at the ballpark. Crosley turned the Reds, who had been perennial losers since their tainted 1919 World Series victory, into steady contenders. In 1938, Crosley hired Bill McKechnie, a proven winner, to manage the team. McKechnie turned the club around in a flash.

In the 1930s and early 1940s, horse racing was one of the most popular spectator sports in Cincinnati and many other major cities in the United States. *Courtesy of Public Library of Cincinnati and Hamilton County.*

In 1939, the team thrilled its hometown fans by winning the National League Pennant only to be crushed by the New York Yankees in the World Series, 4–0. The core of the team returned in 1940, elevating and renewing the expectations of fans hoping for a return to the October Classic. During the 1940 season, the Reds would attract an average of more than ten thousand fans per game. When the Reds left town to play scheduled road games, semiprofessional teams that played in the Negro Leagues hosted games before smaller, but appreciative, African American crowds at Crosley Field. While the Reds were the unquestionable top draw in town, other sports had also become popular. On crisp, cool nights in the spring and summer, fans also enjoyed horse racing at River Downs. During the balmy autumn weekends and colder wintry ones, fans flocked to the campuses of Xavier University and the University of Cincinnati to watch collegiate football.

Moviegoers patronized seven downtown theaters. For those Cincinnatians who craved outdoor forms of recreation, the city boasted more than 150 parks. Urban folk flocked to band concerts, hiking trails and botanical displays at the Krohn Conservatory in Eden Park. Another favorite weekend destination for Cincinnatians was the amusement park Coney Island, which was adjacent to River Downs. Named for its famous counterpart in New York City, the amusement park located east of the city had entertained guests since the turn of the century. While it was possible to travel by car

Most families traveled to Coney Island aboard the *Island Queen*. Boarding from the public landing downtown, the upriver journey took about an hour. *Courtesy of Public Library of Cincinnati and Hamilton County.*

to Coney Island, most patrons traveled ten miles upriver from the public landing downtown, via the *Island Queen*. Thirty-five cents (only twenty cents for children) covered the cost of transportation *and* admission to the park! Guests typically enjoyed a day of swimming, amusement park rides and other attractions and perhaps a night punctuated with dancing to the sounds of big bands at Moonlight Gardens.

Many of the city's cultural institutions had developed national reputations that belied its proud parochialism. Patrons of the arts frequented Music Hall to see top-caliber performances by the Cincinnati Symphony Orchestra, under the baton of conductor Eugene Goosens. During the summer months, many of the same people took in performances by the Cincinnati Opera at the Cincinnati Zoological Gardens. NBC had been broadcasting the performances since the 1920s. Cincinnatians demonstrated an appreciation for local talent and helped foster it over the years. The Art Museum in Eden Park also housed an Art Academy. Charles P. Taft and his wife, Anna, donated their home to the city in 1927 with more than six hundred art treasures; the Taft Museum opened its doors to city visitors in 1932.

Like many cities in the United States, Cincinnati had developed a rich and diverse tradition of church life. Protestants had been among the first wave of

This page and opposite: Cincinnati enjoyed a wide range of cultural outlets. The Cincinnati Zoological and Botanical Gardens, formed in 1875, was the second-oldest zoo in the United States (above). Cincinnati's Music Hall, located on Central Parkway, just north of downtown, became the permanent home of the Cincinnati Symphony Orchestra in 1936 (below). The Taft Museum, located in Lytle Place, represented one of the city's hidden treasures (opposite). *Courtesy of Public Library of Cincinnati and Hamilton County*.

immigrants to come to the river city. Nearly every mainline denomination found a home in some corner of the frontier city. One of the most durable and prominent congregations to take root in the city was the Christ Episcopal Church. Founded in 1818 by William Henry Harrison and Daniel Drake, the Fourth Street location enabled it to minister to the city's needy and poor in

the working-class quarters. Around the same time, many German and Irish Catholics poured into Cincinnati. The Catholic population grew so rapidly that by 1821, the Archdiocese of Cincinnati was established. By 1940, the boundaries of the archdiocese encompassed the better part of southwestern Ohio. German Jews also immigrated to the Queen City. The first synagogue constructed downtown was K.K. Bene Israel at the intersection of Sixth Street and Broadway in 1836. Over the next eighty years or so, Jews in Cincinnati moved out of the inner-city neighborhoods into areas such as Avondale and created new church communities in the process.

Those younger city residents who felt inclined to attend college had several options from which to choose. The biggest magnet for potential students by 1940 was the University of Cincinnati (UC). Established in 1819 as Cincinnati College, the school had relocated to Clifton and blossomed into a large, coeducational municipal university by the 1870s. Spread out over a sprawling fifty-six-acre campus sandwiched between Burnett Woods and the communities of Corryville and Clifton Heights, UC boasted a student population of about 11,500. The university employed about six hundred faculty members. Over the years, it developed a national reputation for its cooperative education model used predominantly by its Engineering and Business Colleges. One of the newest additions to the campus in 1940 was its building to house activities related to the Reserve Officers' Training Corps. The U.S. Army had developed a presence on many major college campuses in the mid-1930s. UC students practiced military drills and learned how to handle firearms. Others participated in antiaircraft gunnery practice.

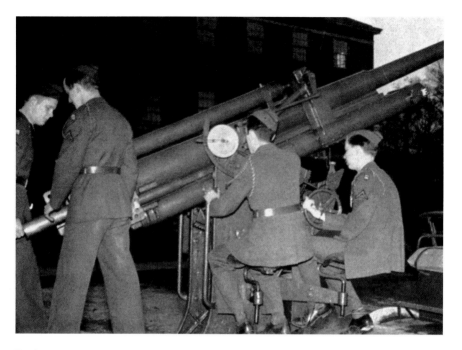

During the 1930s, one of the ROTC groups on the University of Cincinnati campus practiced martial drills with an antiaircraft gun. *Courtesy of University of Cincinnati Archives.*

Located just three miles to the northeast on Victory Parkway in Evanston stood Xavier University. It was a much smaller school that was run by and operated under the auspices of Jesuit priests for the Roman Catholic Church. Founded in 1831, Xavier attracted fewer than 1,000 students. Concerned about sagging enrollments, university officials introduced ROTC training into its curriculum in 1935 and made military drilling mandatory for its students in 1938.

While it is fair to say a martial climate resided on these campuses long before war in Europe began, school officials at Hebrew Union College (HUC), just down the road from UC, demonstrated a different sort of heightened awareness about the war in Europe. Founded in 1875, by Rabbi Isaac M. Wise, HUC was a tiny school with a student population of about fifty. No ROTC units drilled on its campus. Instead, its officials were spurred into action by Germany's anti-Semitic policies. As early as 1934, HUC president Julian Morgenstern helped relocate several German Jewish scholars who had lost their jobs as a result of discriminatory policies in Nazi Germany.

Politically, the city had long been under the sway of the Republican Party. Since the end of the Civil War, Ohioans had elected four of the state's own

In the late 1930s, Hebrew Union College president Julian Morgenstern (seated at table, right center) helped arrange for the rescues of several Jewish scholars from Nazi Germany. *Courtesy of American Jewish Archives.*

citizens to the presidency. No other state could make a comparable claim. With few exceptions, Republican voters turned out to support their candidates on election day in contests involving national and statewide offices. The city boasted three monuments to martyred Republican presidents: two that were dedicated to Abraham Lincoln and one to James Garfield. If more proof of their conservative bona fides was needed, Cincinnatians could also point with pride to their favorite son, William Howard Taft, the nation's twenty-fifth president (1909–13), who was born in Mount Auburn.

At the local level, the political picture looked entirely different. Republican Party officials who dominated city affairs had tarnished the city's good name and image. From the 1880s until the mid-1920s, the Queen City was in the grasp of a powerful and corrupt machine run by George "Boss" Cox. The city's infrastructure had been neglected. Its finances were in shambles. The city had exhausted all of the approved funds on the failed subway project. Republicans controlled thirty-one of the thirty-two seats on the unwieldy city council. In 1924, Murray Seasongood, a young and ambitious Republican reformer, introduced an initiative on the ballot to create a new form of

Avondale Public School and Lincoln
Monument,
Cincinnati, Ohio.

This page and opposite: Charles P. Taft commissioned the beardless statue of Abraham Lincoln in Lytle Park, just outside the Taft Museum. His brother, former president William Howard Taft, dedicated the statue on March 31, 1917. Several years earlier, Charles Clinton, a Civil War veteran and sculptor, donated a bronze statue of the "Great Emancipator" to Rockdale Elementary School. Cincinnati paid tribute to another martyred president, Ohio's James Garfield. The statue originally occupied the busy intersection of Eighth and Race Streets from 1887 until 1915, when it was moved to Garfield Place. *Courtesy of Public Library of Cincinnati and Hamilton County.*

municipal government. A new method of proportional representation allowed for the election of nine council members, who, in turn, would choose a mayor to serve a two-year term. Since Cox's corrupt reign stemmed from his grip on the mayor's office, the mayor's duties under the charter form of government would be limited to a largely ceremonial role. The real business of day-to-day government would fall on a newly created administrator, the city manager. Seasongood served as the city's first charter mayor from 1926 to 1930. He convinced Lieutenant Colonel Clarence O. Sherrill, a former West Point graduate and decorated veteran of the Great War, to serve as Cincinnati's first city manager. Sherrill had experience working directly under Presidents Harding and Coolidge. As the director of Public Buildings and Parks in Washington, D.C., he had supervised the construction of the Lincoln Memorial. The two men helped transform Cincinnati from a cesspool of political corruption to a model of good and efficient government in a few short years. Progressive Charterites governed the city through most of the Depression decade. Russell Wilson, who had worked as a theater critic and assistant editor of the *Times-Star*, succeeded Seasongood as mayor, serving from 1932 until 1938.

These political reforms were not welcomed by all local Republicans in Cincinnati and Hamilton County. Stalwart conservatives, like Robert A.

Taft, the oldest son of former president William Howard Taft, opposed Seasongood's reforms. His younger brother, Charles P. Taft Jr., who sided with the Charter Party, endorsed the reforms. In 1938, party regulars won back the majority of seats in the council election. They chose James Garfield Stewart, who had served on council since 1934, to be the next mayor, a position he held until 1944.

At some point in his career as a humorist and syndicated columnist, Will Rogers once observed, "All I know is what I read in the newspapers," or something to that effect. If that were true for average Cincinnatians in 1940, they likely would have been keeping their eyes on one of two stories that unfolded that year. One story involved the political ambitions and fortunes (or misfortunes) of Cincinnati's most famous resident, Robert A. Taft, one of Ohio's U.S. senators. After only two years of service as Ohio's junior senator, Taft announced his intention to seek the nomination of his party for president. At first blush, the campaign seemed brilliant. Republicans had suffered under the not-so-distant memories of Herbert Hoover. Party leaders welcomed Taft's instant name recognition and fresh face. Early in 1940, polls showed Taft—along with Senator Arthur Vandenberg of Michigan and Thomas Dewey, New York City's young and energetic prosecuting attorney—as one of the frontrunners for the nomination.

During the campaign, Taft stumbled early and often. He failed to take much notice of the alarming events in Europe. He had hoped to wage a campaign against the New Deal and run on economic issues. When he did venture to make comments about the global crisis on the Senate floor, Taft usually voiced concerns about the administration's desire to involve the United States in Europe's war. Taft's isolationist views matched the temperament of a broad swath of midwesterners. Moderate Republicans in the Northeast, unlike Taft, favored closer ties with Great Britain. Those intraparty differences came to the fore on June 2, 1940, when Taft and his wife, Martha, were invited to a dinner hosted by Ogden Reid, a wealthy and prominent publisher of an internationalist New York newspaper. The Tafts quickly discovered that they were in the minority. Among the guests was Lord Lothian, the British ambassador to the United States, and Wendell Willkie, an Indiana industrialist and ambitious political outsider who had never held elective office. When the assembled dinner guests began making impromptu toasts praising the British heroes who risked their lives defending their country, Taft erupted. He informed the startled onlookers: "I had not intended to take any part in this discussion, but I feel that I cannot sit here and let my silence be interpreted as agreement." A lively shouting match ensued before the Tafts took their leave. If Taft had trouble controlling his temper in private settings with potential donors, he seemed to exhibit the very opposite problem of not demonstrating any passion at all when he was on the campaign trail. Voters had trouble warming to Taft's seemingly aloof presence. To his credit, the young senator could argue complicated policy points before crowds, but he seemed unable or unwilling to make much of a personal connection with average folks. Frankly, many voters saw him as something of a "cold fish." At the Republican National Convention, Wendell Willkie surged ahead of Taft and Dewey to capture the nomination. Taft finished a distant second in the balloting; through his lieutenants, he made it clear that he had zero interest in becoming Willkie's running mate. Ever the party loyalist, Taft quickly shelved his disappointment and agreed to campaign for Willkie. If nothing else, it gave Taft another opportunity to thwart President Roosevelt in his quest for an unprecedented third term.

The second story that vied for Cincinnatians' attention had everything to do with the Cincinnati Reds. They were quietly putting together another impressive season under manager Bill McKechnie. His players called him "the Deacon" because of his teetotaling ways and his aversion to profanity. McKechnie was lucky enough to have the services of Bucky Walters and Paul Derringer as his one-two punch for solid pitching, which was complemented by the hard-throwing and sometimes erratic Johnny Vandermeer, who had already made a name for himself in franchise and major-league history by throwing back-to-back no-hitters in the 1938 season. Slugger and first baseman Frank McCormick supplied most of the offense for the Reds.

Part of the magic of this season for its fans had to do with the adversity that the team was forced to overcome. In August, backup catcher Willard Hershberger committed suicide. Hershberger had been with the team since the 1938 season. He found himself trapped in an age where it was not acceptable to discuss mental illness problems in public. After an August 2 doubleheader, Hershberger unburdened himself to McKechnie, revealing the extent of his lifelong anguish. When he was eighteen years old, he had made the painful discovery that his father had taken his own life. Hershberger was never able to come to terms with that trauma.

Team officials discovered the catcher's body in his hotel room. The team retired Hershberger's jersey and dedicated the remainder of its season to his memory.

By October 1940, the Reds realized their goal to return to the World Series. For the first time in franchise history, the Reds won one hundred games during their exciting season. After defeating the Brooklyn Dodgers to capture the league championship, the Reds went back to the World Series, where they defeated the Detroit Tigers in seven games. Paul Derringer pitched the final out. That night, a massive celebration erupted. Pedestrians flooded the downtown area and celebrated at Fountain Square throughout the night. In a truly magnanimous gesture immediately after the game, the Reds players voted to pool a portion of their postseason earnings to give to Walter Hershberger's widow. A few weeks after the World Series concluded, Frank McCormick learned that sportswriters had voted him the most valuable player of the National League. It was the third consecutive year that a Reds player had been named league MVP.

Global events in 1940 had a way of trumping local stories, even when those local stories garnered national attention, like the favorite son Taft candidacy and the hometown Reds. The pages of Raymond Walters's diary reflect the struggles of one erudite Cincinnatian to balance and compartmentalize his interest in global affairs and stories more directly related to Cincinnati. Walters, an avid Reds fan, enjoyed recounting the successes of his hometown team during the pennant race and postseason. Occasionally, he and one of his sons attended home games at Crosley Field. As the war intensified, Walters paid more and more attention to the daily troop movements of Allied and Axis forces than topics concerning domestic politics and sports.

The story that slowly took over the front pages and top stories on radio broadcasts told of the epic struggles that were being waged each day in Europe and Asia. Within a matter of months, Hitler's forces had overrun the vast majority of western Europe and parts of Scandinavia. President Roosevelt worried what a Nazi-dominated Europe would mean for the United States. Roosevelt faced an uphill battle with isolationist critics in Congress. During the Depression, appropriations for national defense had been cut drastically. In 1940, the U.S. Army ranked seventeenth in the world behind such nonentities as Portugal.

The Roosevelt administration jolted the country out of its peacetime mode of operation and began to harness the nation's industrial resources for what it euphemistically referred to as a defense buildup, or mobilization. Such euphemisms were important for a country that was still officially neutral. On May 16, 1940, FDR asked Congress for an appropriation of nearly $1 billion for defense spending that included the ambitious goal of manufacturing fifty thousand airplanes. The president soberly assessed the deteriorating situation in Europe and explained how those conditions posed potential dangers for the western hemisphere. He warned: "These are ominous days—days whose swift and shocking developments force every neutral nation to look to its defenses in the light of new factors."

The president reminded members of Congress that in a bygone era (the War of 1812), when ships only averaged five miles per hour, a powerful enemy navy was able to reach our nation's shores and torch our Capitol. The United States, FDR argued, was equally or more vulnerable in this new era of modern warfare. If Germany was able to establish air bases in the West Indies, for example, enemy planes could reach American targets in Florida in a matter of minutes. Similarly, West Coast cities such as Seattle and San Francisco could be vulnerable to enemy air attacks if Alaska or portions of Canada fell into the wrong hands. The president continued:

> Our task is plain. The road we must take is clearly indicated. Our defenses must be invulnerable, our security absolute. But our defense as it was yesterday, or even as it is today, does not provide security against potential developments and dangers of the future.
>
> Defense cannot be static. Defense must grow and change from day to day. Defense must be dynamic and flexible, an expression of the vital forces of the nation and of its resolute will to meet whatever challenge the future may hold. For these reasons, I need hardly assure you that after the adjournment of this session of the Congress, I will not hesitate to call the Congress into special session if at any time the situation of the national defense requires it. The Congress and the Chief Executive constitute a team where the defense of the land is concerned.

The federal government had already started awarding contracts through the War and Navy Departments to suitable industries. In July, Wright Aeronautical Corporation, a New Jersey–based aircraft manufacturer, announced its intention to build a new plant in Lockland, twelve miles north of Cincinnati, that would manufacture aircraft engines. Wright officials cited the strength of vocational education in the city's public schools, the concentration of machine tools and the harmonious relations between labor and management as compelling reasons for choosing a Cincinnati location. Plans for a new four-lane super highway were announced. The proposed highway would follow the old canal bed that German immigrants had dug along the Mill Creek Valley during the nineteenth century. The new road was modeled after the recently completed Pennsylvania Turnpike, one of the nation's first real highways. In October, city officials broke ground at the new plant site. Cincinnati mayor Stewart, Congressman William E. Hess and Lockland mayor Paul Morrow attended the ribbon-cutting ceremony.

During the summer months, after he accepted the nomination of the Democratic Party for a third term, Roosevelt made two symbolic appointments to his cabinet. He invited Henry L. Stimson, a prominent Republican lawyer who had served as William Howard Taft's secretary of war and Herbert Hoover's secretary of state. FDR also cleared the way for Henry Knox, a Republican newspaper publisher and Alf Landon's running mate in 1936, to join the administration as secretary of the navy. Both men supported the president's policies of supplying aid for Great Britain. Roosevelt used his executive powers to deliver timely aid to the embattled prime minister. He and Churchill agreed to a deal in which the United States transferred fifty destroyers to Great Britain; in return, the United States received long-term leases to naval bases in island possessions controlled by Great Britain in the West Indies. The deal reflected a closer relationship that was developing between the two leaders. Two weeks later, on September 16, 1940, Roosevelt made an even bolder move when he signed the Burke-Wadsworth Act, the first peacetime draft in U.S. history. Men between the ages of twenty-one and thirty-five would be subject to the draft. FDR appointed former Cincinnati city manager Clarence A. Dykstra (1930–36) to serve as the administrator of the Selective Service Administration.

Men eligible for the draft reported to one of the 729 polling precincts, typically the one closest to where they lived, to provide basic information about their age, address and number of dependents. This would help officials manning the 338 local draft boards to determine the status of the potential draftees. Mostly, the registration process proceeded without incident. By late October, more than eighty-one thousand men in Hamilton County had signed up for the draft. Lieutenant Colonel W.H. Curerton, who had been assigned to Cincinnati's Army Recruiting District, explained how draftees, once their number was selected in a lottery system, would report to the induction center at Fort Thomas, Kentucky, for physicals and the administration of the oath of office. On November 15, 1940, the first three men drafted from Cincinnati—Howard B. Hall of Oakley, Paul Vogelsang of Hyde Park and George Schoettinger of Madisonville—received their notices. They were among the first group to cross over to northern Kentucky for their induction ceremonies.

When African Americans in Cincinnati discovered that they would be serving in racially segregated units with white officers, an official practice that dated back to the Mexican War, leaders of twenty-seven different social welfare groups, including the United Council of Negro Organizations, met at the Ninth Street YMCA to air their complaints about the draft. These groups expressed the hope that a democracy such as the United States owed more to its citizens. The *Cincinnati Times-Star* published the leaders' prepared statement, which was addressed to the state director of the selective service. The assembled leaders asserted that

> *the Negro citizen has an unblemished record of meritorious performance and unfaltering loyalty in the military history of the United States. It is the desire and intention of Negro citizens to defend our native country.*
>
> *The Democratic way of life cannot be realized or preserved in America until the Negro citizens are given equal opportunity for training and integration in all phases of the military and the naval forces without the stigma of race discrimination….The anomaly of the vaunted democratic way of life in America is the fact that Negro citizens must protest and fight prejudice in order to obtain the right to fight as free men against a common enemy.*

Sadly, these pleas went unheeded. Black soldiers would be forced to adhere to the age-old patterns of racial discrimination and segregation when they entered into the service of the armed forces. The changes these black organizations envisioned would not occur until 1948, three years after the conclusion of World War II.

The presidential election of 1940 turned out to be exceptional in the sense that it was one of the few such elections that hinged on issues of foreign policy. During this modern era of politics, presidential contests more frequently turned on domestic and economic issues. FDR's decision to push for the Selective Service Act before the election proved to be a sound strategy. Willkie had difficulties conveying to his supporters how his positions on key issues like the draft or the Lend-Lease Act differed from the president's policies.

In mid-October, with the baseball season complete, Wendell Willkie made a final campaign stop in Cincinnati and delivered a speech at Crosley Field before a crowd of about fifteen thousand supporters. A few weeks later, on November 4, Cincinnatians went to the polls to vote. University of Cincinnati president Raymond Walters listened to the president speak on the radio the night before election day: "The President's words are measured, his tone is calm and dignified; there is no overdone bitterness or overdone dramatics such as had marred earlier addresses…Now he is reading a prayer. Very effective. It will not however change my vote."

FDR did not have the same phenomenal showing he had registered in his landslide victory in 1936. Still, his returns were impressive. The president garnered close to five million more votes than Wendell Willkie. His electoral victory was even more impressive. While he failed to carry Cincinnati—it was the only city with a population greater than 400,000 that did not vote Democratic—Roosevelt did manage to carry Hamilton County and the state of Ohio. Two days later, a despondent Walters, still lamenting the election day results, confided in his diary:

> to the millions of the adherents of Wendell Willkie such as myself, this has been a bitter experience. The outcome seems to me…to be more of a manifestation of the world-wide impulse of peoples to seek economic security by following a leader who promises it to them in positive and glowing terms. The German people flocked to Hitler; and the French appear anxious for strong control on similar terms of subservience.

Churchill, of course, welcomed the news of Roosevelt's victory. A newly elected Willkie administration might have cast doubt on the level of support the United States was willing to extend to Great Britain. As it stood by the end of 1940, Churchill's wartime ministry had nearly bankrupted its resources in its desperate defense during the London Blitz and the counterattacks the British waged on German cities. At a December 17 press conference, the president laid out a plan that would allow the United States to circumvent the "cash and carry" provision of the neutrality act to offer massive material aid to Great Britain. Roosevelt offered the following analogy:

> Suppose my neighbor's home catches fire, and I have a length of garden hose four or five hundred feet away. If he can take my garden hose and connect it up with his hydrant, I may help him to put out his fire…I don't say to him before that operation, "Neighbor, my garden hose cost me $15; you

*have to pay me $15 for it"...I don't want $15—I want my garden hose
back after the fire is over.*

Twelve days later, in one of his fireside chats, FDR further discussed the
idea of increased aid to Great Britain to radio listeners across the nation. He
instructed his audience that Great Britain did not want the United States to
fight its war. What it needed were the tools and supplies. The United States,
FDR urged, had an opportunity to be "an arsenal for democracy." Critics
of the president quickly countered with their views. Any increase in aid to
Britain, they argued, would only accelerate the path of American entry into
Europe's war.

Before the end of the year arrived, the war had made its presence felt
on a smaller segment of Cincinnati's population. Those who had paid
attention to the war in Europe learned that the Nazi armies had received
critical support from collaborators and fifth columnists to help speed up
Nazi domination of the Continent. In May 1940, Congress enacted the
Smith Act, also known as the Alien Registration Act. This law required
immigrants of German descent in the United States to register with local
law enforcement officials. One month later, the Roosevelt administration
transferred the Immigration and Naturalization Service (INS), which had
been under the auspices of the Labor Department, to the Department of
Justice. This jurisdictional move signaled a critical shift in the thinking of
at least some administration officials who now viewed alien residents as a
potential threat to the nation's internal security. In September, the *Times-
Star* advised Cincinnati residents of German descent that they would be
required to register their permanent addresses with the U.S. Postal Office
before the end of December. By the time the mandate was implemented,
Italy and Japan had formalized their respective alliances with Nazi
Germany. The Tri-Partite Act of September 1940 led to the recognition
of the Axis powers. This meant that Cincinnati enemy aliens of German,
Italian and Japanese descent (there were only a handful of this latter
group) had to register their addresses and place their fingerprints on file
with the INS office downtown.

As Cincinnatians looked toward a new year, they were uncertain what
the future held in store for them. Germany continued to threaten the one
remaining democracy, Great Britain, in Europe. Russia had consolidated
its grip on the Baltic states. Japan used every weapon at its disposal to
increase its control over mainland China. If the United States were to
adopt the role suggested by the president and become "the arsenal for

democracy," how would that affect the nation's neutral status? Could the United States increase aid to Great Britain without increasing the likelihood that it would enter the war as a belligerent nation? These were questions on the minds of many Cincinnatians, and they would soon be debated in earnest across the country and around the world.

Chapter 2

TORN APART

A City Divided by the War, 1941

President Roosevelt gave the nation its marching orders in December 1940. His "arsenal of democracy" speech made clear his position on the war in Europe. The United States, he believed, had an obligation to help defend Great Britain in its fight against Nazi Germany. By defending democracy on the British shores, America would be safeguarding its own national security interests. The president's plan to assist Great Britain more earnestly only demonstrated how much his positions on foreign policy had evolved over the past few years. In 1936, the president gave an address to a crowd in Chautauqua, New York, which is best known for his famous quip: "I hate war." Yet even in that speech, he had left himself some wiggle room declaring: "We are not isolationists except in so far as we seek to isolate ourselves completely from war. Yet we must remember that so long as war exists on earth there will be some danger that even the Nation which most ardently desires peace may be drawn into war."

During those four years since the Chautauqua address, conditions in Europe had deteriorated so rapidly and so profoundly that public opinion in the United States had reversed itself and supported most of the president's initiatives concerning the nation's defense buildup, aid to Great Britain and, most notably, the need for the draft.

Critics of Roosevelt's interventionist foreign policy views had suffered one embarrassing defeat after another, including Franklin Roosevelt's 1940 reelection to an unprecedented third term. Perhaps sensing that the election was a foregone matter, grass-roots isolationists and anti-interventionist critics began to work in league with one another in order to oppose the president more effectively. That September, while Congress hashed out the details of the Destroyers for Bases deal and the Selective Service Act, a little-known group of Yale University students invited famed aviator Charles Lindbergh to kick off a lecture series devoted to current events. By the fall of 1941, Lindbergh's reputation as a controversial public figure in the conversation about America's role in Europe's war had been well established. These young anti-interventionists at Yale formed the first student-led chapter of the America First Committee (AFC), a group that would quickly become one of the most powerful interest groups to oppose FDR's foreign policy. The group's charter members read like a "who's who" of future notable public servants, including Gerald Ford, Sargent Shriver, Cyrus Vance and Potter Stewart. Stewart happened to be the eldest son of Cincinnati mayor James G. Stewart.

In his Yale address, Lindbergh minimized the threat of enemy air attacks from Europe or Asia on American targets. He criticized the Roosevelt administration for pushing the country to a wartime footing. Finally, he acknowledged the student anti-interventionists at Yale and expressed the hope that college students across the nation would make their opinions heard in this vital debate. The AFC quickly took root. The Yale organization was soon subsumed by a larger group of prominent midwestern isolationists. Chicago, rather than New Haven, Connecticut, became the epicenter for isolationist politics. The AFC created a national board of directors that included Robert Wood, the CEO of Sears and Roebuck, and Robert McCormick, the publisher and owner of the *Chicago Tribune*. While Senators Burton K. Wheeler (Democrat, Montana) and Gerald P. Nye (Republican, North Dakota) officially joined as members, their fellow isolationist colleague in the Senate, Robert Taft, refused to join, even though he supported the core values of the organization.

AFC chapters cropped up mostly in the Midwest. While the heaviest concentration of its activities lay within a two-hundred-mile radius of Chicago, Cincinnati proved to be fertile ground for the AFC. On February 21, organizers in the Queen City announced the formation of the Metropolitan Cincinnati Chapter of the AFC. The acerbic Alice Roosevelt Longworth, wife of former Speaker of the House Nicholas Longworth and daughter of former president Theodore Roosevelt, agreed to serve as the group's honorary chairperson. She also held a seat on the national AFC's board of directors. The day-to-day responsibilities of the local chapter were shouldered by J. Austin White, a twenty-eight-year-old businessman who ran his own investment firm.

At about the same time, the formation of a Cincinnati chapter of a pro-interventionist group, the Committee to Defend America by Aiding Its Allies (CDAAA), set the stage for a vigorous foreign policy discussion. Since the spring of 1940, the CDAAA—also known as the White Committee, named after its spokesman, newspaper journalist William Allen White—had supported the early efforts of the Roosevelt administration to assist Great Britain. Cincinnati city councilman Charles P. Taft, Senator Taft's younger brother, turned down an offer to head up the Cincinnati chapter. That honor eventually went to former mayor and city councilman Russell Wilson. The two groups vied for headlines in the daily newspapers. Each group urged fellow Cincinnatians to make their voices heard in Washington.

From the AFC's headquarters at 330 Walnut Street, Allen White sent out a mailer to the group's members that contained a scripted plea entitled the "Relaxer's Creed." The AFC manifesto employed sarcasm and reverse psychology to motivate its members to write letters to their congressmen and senators to urge repeal of the proposed legislation:

> *If you want war—just relax, you'll get it.*
> *Don't telegraph your Senators, Congressmen and the President. Telegrams, telephone calls and postage costs money.*
> *A boy's life isn't worth the call…*
> *You can always duck into the doorway to avoid looking into the eyes of a draftee. He will never know you failed him and are sending him to his death.*

For the next several weeks, Congress debated the proposed lend-lease bill. Roosevelt's aides, working with Democrat leaders in the House of Representatives, wanted to make sure everything was done to ensure its passage. The lend-lease bill appeared on the docket of upcoming legislation as House Resolution (H.R.) 1776. Lindbergh predictably testified against the bill before the House Committee on Foreign Affairs. Taft fought the measure on the Senate floor. On March 11, 1941, FDR signed the bill into law.

Roosevelt's legislative victory essentially marked the unofficial end of American neutrality. Despite the president's assurances to the contrary, passage of the bill pushed the United States closer to war. Increased trade with Great Britain meant that the United States would assume a greater role in protecting the British convoys crossing the Atlantic. Local repercussions were inevitable Cincinnatians realized as they contemplated changing events. Senator Taft's wife, Martha had long supported women's organizations that worked for world peace and disarmament. However, when the League of

Women Voters reversed its position and gave its support to the passage of the Lend-Lease Act, Mrs. Taft publicly resigned her membership and devoted her energies to supporting the AFC.

The great debate continued. The national AFC and its local chapters modified their complaints about the Roosevelt administration after lend-lease became a reality. The new point of contention was Roosevelt's willingness to deploy the U.S. Merchant Marines to assist in convoying supplies to Great Britain. In late April, Austin White's AFC group petitioned the Cincinnati City Council to display five coffins on the esplanade near Fountain Square. The purpose of the event was to "demonstrate our educational program of keeping our beloved country out of war." On May 3, the AFC unveiled its display to the city. It placed crude, handmade black coffins, each with a placard. The display was designed to stop passersby in their tracks. One sign read: "Don't Put Your Baby in a Box—Join the America First Committee." Another one said: "Write or Wire the President: No Convoys. No Patrols. No War." Large crowds of downtown shoppers and workers congregated around the square for hours.

Above and opposite: Members of the local chapter of the America First Committee placed faux caskets around Fountain Square to express their opposition to President Roosevelt's decision to provide military aid to Great Britain. *Courtesy of American Jewish Archives.*

Five days later, city hall became the next battleground between pro-interventionists and anti-interventionists. The city council chambers were buzzing with activity related to the antiwar display. Russell Wilson, who had been absent the day the AFC asked the council for a permit, lambasted Stewart for allowing such a "tasteless demonstration" to take place. Unable to contain his temper, Wilson referred to the AFC as a "pro-Nazi" group repeatedly during his remarks. "I don't think that Cincinnati has been so shocked for a long time," Wilson complained. He added, "It was the sort of thing to please Hitler." Stewart denied any direct involvement with or connection to the AFC. Still, the mayor defended the organization's actions against Wilson's charges, stating that "there are some high grade citizens who have bullet wounds from the last war who belong to that committee." The publicity stunt had worked. Two months after the passage of the Lend-Lease Act, Cincinnatians were still debating the wisdom of increasing aid to Great Britain, especially if it meant inching closer to direct involvement in Europe's war.

Other groups besides Russell Wilson's CDAAA suspected that the AFC harbored pro-Nazi sympathies. Shortly after the war in Europe began, concerned Jews in Cincinnati formed the Jewish Community Relations

The city council chambers were the stage for a volatile debate between isolationists and interventionists in early May 1941. *Courtesy of Public Library of Cincinnati and Hamilton County.*

Committee (JCRC) to monitor the activities of German organizations they suspected might be pro-Nazi. Throughout the 1930s, Jewish refugees had trickled into Cincinnati with stories of their mistreatment at the hands of the Nazis. The JCRC acted as a watchdog, calling attention to groups that expressed open allegiance to Hitler, espoused anti-Semitism or both. Despite Cincinnati's long history of proud ethnic associations with rich traditions of service to their memberships, Cincinnati's German population could not ignore events in Europe, even at the price of polarizing its Christian and Jewish populations. When it was possible, the JCRC sent representatives to public meetings of German societies and organizations whose loyalties it questioned and compiled confidential reports about the meetings.

One local antiwar group that attracted the JCRC's attention called itself the Mothers of Sons. Formed in January 1940, the group attracted fifty to one hundred members at weekly meetings. Although modest in numbers, Mothers of Sons boasted a mailing list of more than fifty thousand. Its original objective was to put pressure on lawmakers to vote against the conscription bill in Congress. It collected sixty-five thousand signatures against the conscription bill. As the war progressed and the Roosevelt administration responded with its national defense buildup, the Mothers of Sons adjusted its critique of the federal government to oppose lend-lease and finally to work against U.S. entry into the war in Europe. As an ultra-conservative group, its message had some constants. Its rhetoric was anti-Roosevelt, anti-British and anti-Jewish.

Eleven days after the AFC coffin demonstration, Mothers of Sons invited anti-interventionists in Cincinnati to the Garden Ballroom on the rooftop of the Hotel Gibson to observe Mother's Day. This meeting marked the first time that various anti-interventionist groups allowed their representatives to sit on the same stage. Until this mass rally, the AFC had taken pains to maintain its distance from other groups that might confuse its message. On May 11, the Mothers of Sons arranged to have Catherine Curtis, a popular and incendiary speaker, address the gathering. Curtis's speeches and writings were usually laced with anti-Semitic and anti-Communist messages. After the singing of the national anthem, she joked with the audience, offering a tongue-in-cheek apology for her tardy arrival. In a not-so-subtle dig at lend-lease, she told the crowd that she had trouble getting a flight to Cincinnati, suggesting that entire warehouses of American airplanes were sitting idle in Great Britain. She stated that only a small minority of Americans on the eastern seaboard favored aiding Great Britain, at which point, several members in the crowd yelled out, "You know it is the Jews!" She compared the current state of divided public opinion to the challenges that divided Americans during the Revolutionary War:

> *Just as in the days of the American Revolution when the Tories were sitting in New York and Philadelphia royally entertained by the British, your ancestors, and I know mine, were fighting and starving accepting meager handouts of grain from the Indians of New York state. How can anyone call me a Nazi when I am speaking for my country…I am giving everything I've got, my time, what little money I have, my energy, to keep the U.S.A. a republic, free and independent, and from becoming again a British colony.*

Cincinnati proved to be a regular stopping point for some prominent Roosevelt critics. In June, Senator Gerald P. Nye appeared with Mrs. Taft at an AFC rally held at Carthage Fair Grounds, just north of the city. The president's supporters picketed the event. Some of the protesters held signs that criticized Senator Taft for sending his wife as an unofficial proxy. A sign read: "Senator Taft Hides Behind a Woman's Petticoat." Nye's speech consisted mostly of anti-British tirades. According to the JCRC reporter monitoring the event, Nye's speech had "no unkind words for Hitler, but many for Churchill, Roosevelt and Willkie. He referred to Willkie as a 'grasshopper statesman' and thereby nearly brought down the stands."

On the other hand, those Cincinnatians who supported the president's policies were not shy about expressing their opinions. By June, Russell Wilson's CDAAA group had yielded the spotlight to a more strident interventionist group, the Fight for Freedom (FFF) Committee, which called for America's immediate armed entry into Europe's war. Episcopal bishop Henry Wise Hobson of the Southern Diocese of Ohio served as the chair of this New York–based organization. A Cincinnati FFF committee set up a downtown office at 720 Vine Street. One FFF poster offered this grim assessment: "The hot breath of Nazi tyrants is already upon us. We must strike at them now and strike with all our force." While FFF might have struck some Cincinnatians as a new voice in the national debate, the parishioners at Christ Church had received regular doses of anti-Hitler screeds in the form of sermons and church bulletin articles from Hobson. One woman wrote to him complaining about the political nature of most of his sermons. The fiery Bishop shot back: "When I face a situation in which all the values which the Christian religion seeks to establish in the life of a man are threatened with denial and destruction I can never shut my eyes [n]or stop my mouth."

Bishop Henry Wise Hobson, the titular head of the Episcopal Diocese of Southern Ohio, became one of the first national leaders to support armed intervention in Europe. *Courtesy of Christ Church Cathedral Archives.*

Due in part to the national stature of FFF, Hobson's remarks in the Queen City attracted the notice of distant critics and supporters alike. The arch-isolationist *Chicago Tribune* berated the bishop for his prowar views. On the other hand, Melvyn Douglas and Helen Gahagan Douglas, husband and wife Hollywood stars and friends of First Lady Eleanor Roosevelt, wrote Hobson expressing their support for the FFF.

Most of the nation's great debate had been focused on whether or not the United States should stand by its ally, Great Britain. The war in Europe and America's potential participation in it grew more complicated as summer approached. On June 22, Hitler shattered his uneasy truce with Joseph Stalin and launched a frontal assault on the Soviet Union. Code named "Operation Barbarossa," the Nazi strike changed the entire dynamic of Europe's war. Now, suddenly, the Soviet Union was fighting for its survival

Serving as archbishop of the Archdiocese of Cincinnati, Reverend John T. McNicholas had been a consistent critic of Joseph Stalin and communism. The onset of war in Europe in 1939 and the passage of the Lend-Lease Act in 1941 did little to soften those views. *Courtesy of Archdiocese of Cincinnati Archives.*

and attracting the sympathy of many American interventionists. Soon, Congress determined that the Soviets would be eligible to receive lend-lease assistance. For many isolationists and anti-interventionists, this development proved a particularly bitter pill. Ever since the war began, Cincinnati's Archbishop McNicholas had been hard pressed to discern the dangers of communism and Nazism. In his frequent articles in the *Catholic Telegraph*, the archbishop consistently argued that opposition to God—whether of a Nazi or a Soviet ilk—represented a greater threat to humanity than war itself.

At some point after the controversial coffin display in early May, the balance of public opinion over these issues began to change. Increasingly, it became clear that the isolationists represented a small but vocal and persistent minority. The majority of Queen City residents began to adjust to the new demands that the national defense buildup was imposing on the city.

Meanwhile, defense contracts continued to roll into Cincinnati. The machine tool industry, as a whole, profited. Aircraft engine production represented another boom industry for the city. The high unemployment rates that defined the Depression decade faded. As the demand for skilled workers intensified, Cincinnati's black leaders hoped that employers would open up opportunities on shop floors and assembly lines. Black labor leaders gained the support of black newspapers in midwestern cities such as Chicago, Cincinnati and Pittsburgh. The *Pittsburgh Courier*, a black weekly newspaper, sponsored the National Committee for the Participation of Negroes in National Defense. The committee coordinated some of the earliest mass protests against the color line erected by defense contractors and also fought to desegregate the armed forces. The midwestern coordinator of the national committee was Theodore M. Berry, a black lawyer and Hamilton County assistant prosecutor. He supplied the major black newspapers with evidence of job discrimination in the North and South. He felt that the black press played "a very important role in highlighting the degree to which Negroes were…held on the sidelines." Berry supported those initiatives designed to spotlight persistent racial discrimination among defense employers.

In May 1941, black labor leaders in Washington, D.C., under the leadership of A. Philip Randolph, the president of the Brotherhood of Sleeping Car Porters, threatened to enact a mass march on the nation's capital if the president did not disband the practice of racial segregation in the armed forces and within defense industries. While the president was unwilling to address any demands related to the armed forces, he did issue Executive Order 8802, which dealt with issues of workplace discrimination. He created a new agency, the Fair Employment Practices Committee

(FEPC). The agency would act as an ombudsman, listening to and hopefully resolving or mitigating complaints about racial discrimination in the workplace, specifically with plants that had been awarded federal defense contracts. Berry, like many black leaders, hoped FDR's executive order signaled a change in past hiring practices. Many regarded the president's actions as a "second Reconstruction." Unfortunately, the optimism was misplaced. It would take years for some Cincinnati employers to welcome black workers into their plants. African Americans were still regarded as second-class citizens. These unfortunate reminders only offered further proof that Cincinnati was a divided city.

For the vast majority of Queen City residents, the renewed economic activity was a welcome sight. Lockland, the site of the new Wright Aeronautical Plant, became a new hub of activity. Cincinnati city planners devised new bus routes to accommodate workers. Eventually, housing projects were developed near the plant. The Wright plant began production of its fourteen-cylinder Cyclone engine in April and would soon become one of the city's largest employers. The recently completed plant boasted four separate assembly lines and a foundry that was said to be the largest of its kind in the United States. Wright officials formally dedicated the plant on June 12. Among the invited guests were William Knudsen, the former CEO of General Motors and director of the Office of Production Management (OPM), the federal agency in charge of coordinating the production of war material. Orville Wright, the sixty-nine-year-old aviation pioneer, came down from his Dayton home to attend the ceremony as well. Aviation had certainly come a long way since that first flight in Kitty Hawk.

As Cincinnati businesses accepted more contracts from the army and navy, business leaders and city officials became increasingly concerned about devising plans to protect work sites as well as places where people lived and worked. Since 1937, the full horrors of modern warfare had been vividly displayed to Americans through dramatic newsreel footage and radio broadcasts from cities in Europe and Asia that had become front line casualties. On May 20, 1941, the Roosevelt administration created the Office of Civilian Defense (OCD) to help cities and states devise such plans. The OCD was also given the task of promoting national unity by channeling the efforts of volunteers into meaningful activities in their communities. The OCD wanted cities and towns to participate in community-based programs that would boost their morale. In a world in which democracy was under constant siege, the Roosevelt administration felt compelled to promote programs that would reassure participants' faith in its democratic institutions.

In the Queen City, city and county officials responded with enthusiasm to OCD requests. In May 1941, Mayor Stewart named Phillip O. Geier, the head of Cincinnati Milling Company, the director of local defense planning. Mayor Stewart agreed to function as the honorary chairman. City planners asserted that "the citizens of every community have a right to assume that their representative officials have considered every possible provision for their protection and safety against sabotage or any act of war."

During the summer, at the request of the War Department, Cincinnati city manager C.O. Sherrill sent a delegation of fire and police officials to Aberdeen, Maryland, to attend special training on chemical warfare. Sherrill had been given charge of coordinating the city's plans for civilian protection. Much time was spent with mayors and fire and police chiefs from adjacent municipalities in Hamilton County coming up with workable plans, such as countywide blackout drills, to protect neighborhoods and production centers. City leaders also sponsored other activities to engage public support for the defense effort. At the suggestion of the OCD, Cincinnatians participated in the nation's first nationwide salvage drive of scrap aluminum. City officials set up a huge fenced-in area near Fountain Square. Boy Scout troops helped collect scrap in the city's neighborhoods. Residents were encouraged to donate items that were no longer of any use to them. The *Times-Star* reported in July 1941 that Cincinnatians "donated enough (scrap) for five fighter planes." By donating old coffee urns and unwanted pots and pans, the administration hoped ordinary Americans would feel more like stakeholders in the larger efforts of their country.

That September, results of the Gallup Public Opinion Polls revealed just how much levels of support for the administration's defense mobilization had evolved. After respondents weighed in on their opinions about the less pressing issue of daylight saving time in their communities, they were asked three sets of questions that revealed much about the state of the American psyche. When asked, a significant majority of respondents—58.4 percent—felt the United States would enter the war before it ended. A follow-up question, "Some people say that the United States is already in the war. In general, do you agree or disagree?" yielded an almost identical result. Nearly 56 percent felt the nation was already at war. Finally, when the same respondents were asked if it were more important for the United States to remain neutral or to help Great Britain "even at the risk of getting into the war," 63 percent favored giving aid to Great Britain.

Not all Cincinnatians, of course, fell in line with these views. During the fall months, AFC rallies continued to draw significant crowds. Their views matched those expressed by Charles Lindbergh, who had become the preeminent spokesman for the isolationist camp. The national AFC did not always agree with the aviator, but it welcomed the large crowds that showed up wherever he spoke. This strategy eventually backfired when Lindbergh made some contentious remarks, controversial even for him, in Des Moines, Iowa, on September 11, 1941. Lindbergh declared: "The three most important groups who have been pressing this country toward war are the British, the Jewish and the Roosevelt administration." Lindbergh's rhetoric had sharpened and intensified, in part because Roosevelt had taken measures that pushed the country ever closer to the brink of war. On September 4, a Nazi U-boat had fired on the USS *Greer* in the Atlantic. The president thereby authorized American ships "to shoot on sight" any hostile German vessels they might encounter. Lindbergh's decision to target American Jews indicated how desperate his attacks had become. Sadly, anti-Semitism had not been absent from earlier AFC rallies, especially in Cincinnati. But this was the first time the national media took Lindbergh to task for such remarks. Even the *Chicago Tribune* roundly criticized Lindbergh. It is worth noting that Ohio's isolationist senator, Robert Taft, remained silent during the entire controversy.

Taft's relationship with Jews in Cincinnati and Ohio was, to put it mildly, complicated. Taft considered himself a friend to the Jews. Earlier in his career, he had publicly espoused his support for the creation of a Jewish state. While this pleased Zionist leaders in the northern part of the state, most of the Reform Jews in Cincinnati considered themselves Anti-Zionists. Their future lay in improving their circumstances and fortunes in the United States rather than the Holy Lands of the Middle East. Cincinnati Jews were doubly disappointed with Taft for his failure to stand up to Lindbergh. After all, had not Taft taken great pains in the 1940 election to distinguish his isolationist views from the more popular interventionist views of Willkie? In the case of Lindbergh's speech, however, he did nothing, and he said nothing. Perhaps Taft felt Lindbergh represented the last best chance to keep America out of the war, and if it came at the expense of American Jews, so be it.

One week after Lindbergh's bombshell, Senator Nye returned to Cincinnati to address an AFC rally. Nye was greeted at Union Terminal by J. Austin White and other local AFC officials. In remarks prepared for the local press, the senator defended Lindbergh's Des Moines speech. He assured a *Times-Star* reporter, "Those who charge Charles A. Lindbergh as an anti-Semite don't know Lindbergh." That evening, Nye addressed a large rally at the Taft Auditorium in downtown Cincinnati. At the nearby Mayfair Hotel, an overflow crowd listened to speakers to hear Nye's address. Mayor

Stewart arrived at the Taft after all the introductory speakers had finished their remarks. He told the crowd that he had come from a PTA meeting, where he had expressed his hope that "the young generation coming up will have more sense about running the world than we have." He welcomed the keynote speaker. Stewart informed the gathering that the previous day had been the 154th anniversary of the drafting of the U.S. Constitution. That fact opened the door for Stewart to make several remarks about the value of free speech. He complimented the assembly for its efforts to promote peace in such a perilous time. The mayor also pointedly reminded listeners that it was Congress, not the president, that was empowered to declare war. The mayor remained on stage for the duration of Nye's speech.

Lindbergh never made an appearance in Cincinnati. Had he done so, it is fair to say he would have attracted a large and supportive crowd. On October 2, the local AFC chapter hosted another rally at the Taft Auditorium. John Flynn, one of the charter members of the national AFC, was the principal speaker. In his introductory remarks for Flynn, J. Austin White mentioned the fact that Lindbergh was addressing a rally in Fort Wayne the following evening. The mere mention of Lindbergh's name drew thunderous applause. Obviously delighted, White noted, "I have yet to see it fail. Whenever the man's name is mentioned, he draws an ovation."

Despite the entrenched views and vitriolic rhetoric of the local AFC, it is fair to say that most Cincinnatians had arrived at the position that American entry into Europe's war was more of a question of "when" rather than "if." One reflection of that change appeared on the editorial page of UC's student newspaper, the *News Record*, just two days after Flynn addressed the AFC rally downtown. The October 4 editorial stated that it had been the policy of the paper to observe a strict "hands off attitude towards international affairs so long as the paper was operating during a period of comparative normalcy." The editors concluded that "these are far from normal times" due to President Roosevelt's proclamation of a state of national emergency. The editors crafted "a statement of policy" that announced its support for aid to Great Britain and Russia and preached tolerance for those who disagreed with the president's interventionist foreign policy:

> *We believe that the efforts of the national administration to give assistance to all nations fighting fascism are in the best interests of the United States and shall be supported by this paper to the limit of its ability.*
>
> *We consider communism likewise the enemy of democracy, and, while we favor granting all assistance to Soviet Russia in her present struggle*

with Germany, we are in no sense advocating or approving the system of government possessed by that country.

We believe that freedom of the press is not limited to those who agree with our policies. The columns in this paper will continue to be open to all students and faculty…who wish to criticize, compliment or comment upon the policies of either the NEWS RECORD, the university, or the national administration.

During the fall of 1941, many Cincinnatians began publicly expressing their support for the national defense effort. In October, residents of Hamilton County and Cincinnati participated in a mass fund drive that netted more than $211,000, which equates to roughly $3.4 million in 2014. The majority of the proceeds raised were earmarked for the United Service Organization, a nonprofit organization that was formed in January 1941 to provide recreational facilities for soldiers traveling between their homes and military training bases. At the same time, local defense officials launched a registration drive for male and female volunteers aged eighteen and older for training in the fields of firefighting, first aid, emergency communications and the like.

To promote awareness for community-based civilian defense programs, the OCD declared November 10–16 Civilian Defense Week. Cincinnati, it turned out, would share a portion of the national spotlight that week. Throughout the summer of 1941, the First Lady had frequently voiced opinions and concerns about the national civilian defense program in her syndicated newspaper columns and in her public addresses. She advocated using civilian defense programs to reinvigorate communities and to defend democracy at home. Her strong advocacy on the matter eventually led the president to appoint her assistant director in charge of voluntary participation in September 1941.

Prior to that appointment, Mrs. Roosevelt had agreed to visit the Queen City to participate in a lecture series on November 12 that was sponsored by the Isaac M. Wise Temple. Designed to promote and explore better relations between the United States and Latin America, the lecture correlated well with the Roosevelt administration's concerns about shoring up its relations with the Latin American republics. The outbreak of war in Europe only heightened those concerns. The president and his advisors worried that Nazi agents in South America might foment acts of sabotage. Administration officials hoped that Mrs. Roosevelt's lecture on "Cultural Relations between the Americas" would assuage those fears. The First Lady had delivered an earlier lecture for the same series in 1938. It was fortuitous that this visit to Cincinnati coincided with Civilian Defense Week. The First Lady wired the lecture organizers to make sure it was acceptable for her to meet with civilian defense volunteers on the day of her scheduled talk. Before the word became fashionable, Eleanor Roosevelt, it is fair to say, was the consummate multitasker of her generation. She divided her energy and attention among a variety of worthy causes. November 12 was just one of her typical days in her usually frenetic schedule.

On November 12, she arrived by train from Detroit with her personal secretary, Malvina Thompson. Arrangements were made for the First Lady to spend the night in the Presidential Suite of the Netherland Hilton. After first meeting with Cincinnati's Bureau of Volunteers for Services and Defense, Mrs. Roosevelt then conducted a press conference at the hotel to promote a variety of civilian defense programs for housewives. At the conclusion of the press conference, she retired to her room with Thompson for a sandwich and a quick nap.

Because of Mrs. Roosevelt's drawing power as a public speaker, the officials at Isaac M. Wise Temple wisely opted to change the venue to the Emery Auditorium, located downtown. The 1,200-seat auditorium easily sold out. The National Youth Administration orchestra began the festivities that evening by accompanying the Western Hills High School Choir in the national anthem. Rabbi Samuel Wohl, who had served as the organizer of the lecture series, introduced the First Lady. Wohl used the forum to express his unequivocal faith in the United States and its democratic institutions: "On this occasion I give thanks to Providence for the fellowship and friendship we enjoy in this our community and for the manifold blessings in our great democracy. This great gathering stirs the heart, and we thank God for our freedom and Democracy that makes it possible for us to be here, to live without fear, to speak our minds, and to seek truth."

Wohl's lengthy introduction took stock of the challenges in Europe and Asia that were threatening the very tenets of democracy:

> *The present crisis in human history is one that has shaken all things to their very foundation...We have been told to choose between the blessing and the curse, slavery or freedom. If we do not make our own history, it will be others who will make history for us. In a supreme hour, Americans under God can still fashion the forces that shall prevail. May we go forward with confidence that right will win, and the might of evil will be vanquished.*

Following her address, the First Lady was escorted to the Green Room backstage. Mayor Stewart took it upon himself to invite about fifty dignitaries from the city to meet the guest of honor. This reception committee of honored guests was a veritable "who's who" of the Queen City's finest. Top industrialists, all three university presidents, newspaper editors, federal judges, educators, community activists and several elected officials crowded in to greet Mrs. Roosevelt. Among those conspicuously absent were both of Cincinnati's congressional representatives and Senator Taft. Even the First Lady's visit, it appeared, could not unite the divided city.

As mayor of the city, James Garfield Stewart faced a series of difficult choices during the nation's tilt toward war in 1941. On the one hand, Stewart had made no secret about his opposition to aiding Great Britain, even after the Lend-Lease Act passed Congress. He frequently attended AFC rallies in Cincinnati and welcomed many leading isolationist and anti-interventionist critics to the city. On the other hand, he served as the titular head of the Mayor's Committee on Defense from May until mid-November. In that position, he was responsible for assisting federal officials with the national defense effort.

In order to implement those mobilization plans successfully, Stewart had to rely on the cooperation of the thirty-two other municipalities and townships located in Hamilton County. On November 15, Governor John W. Bricker recognized the Hamilton County National Defense Council (HCNDC) as the officially sanctioned local defense organization for Hamilton County and Cincinnati. From that point on, Cincinnati worked in cooperation with this countywide defense council. City manager Sherrill continued to coordinate protective drills for the city, but Mayor Stewart was relieved of duties concerning civilian defense planning. Morris Edwards, a local businessman, assumed those responsibilities as the new HCNDC executive director.

———•—•———

A little more than three weeks after Mrs. Roosevelt's lecture at the Emery Auditorium, the Andrews Sisters were wrapping up a successful multicity tour of the Midwest. The popular singing sisters, Patti, Maxine and LaVerne, were scheduled to perform at the Shubert Theatre with the Joe Venuti Orchestra on December 5, marking the second time they had performed in the Queen City that year. After selling out the shows on Friday and Saturday nights, the manager felt confident the girls would shatter the one-weekend attendance record for the theater. During the past year and a half, the sisters had become nationally known for their hit singles "Boogie Woogie Bugler Boy" and "In Apple Blossom Time." They had also appeared in a series of B movies with comedians Lou Abbott and Bud Costello that showcased their singing talents. More recognition came their way when the U.S. Treasury Department asked the three sisters in October 1941 to record a patriotic song called "Any Bonds Today?" to inspire people to invest in defense bonds.

On Sunday afternoon, December 7, when the three girls walked from their downtown hotel to the Shubert, they noticed that the streets were empty. Maxine recalled the events of that day:

> *I noticed something different when LaVerne, Patty, and I arrived at the Shubert Theater…Every day when we had arrived, there was a long line of people standing on the sidewalk in front of the box office to buy tickets for our first show. It didn't make any difference how cold it was—and in Cincinnati—it gets plenty cold!—or how much snow we might get, people were lined up for blocks. But on that Sunday in 1941, the sidewalks were empty.*

When they entered the theater, stagehands were milling around talking. It was at that point they learned the news that Japan had attacked U.S. naval forces at Pearl Harbor. The girls looked at each other and asked the innocent question that tens of thousands of Americans must have asked over and over that day: "Where is Pearl Harbor?" Many Americans would need to refresh their knowledge of world geography in order to fully understand the implications of this startling news. What people did understand was that the nation was now at war.

Initially, the information trickling in from Hawaii was fragmentary at best. It would take weeks before Americans fully grasped the extent of the destruction and the level of sacrifice that had transpired at Pearl Harbor, Wake Island, Guam and the Philippines. Five battleships were destroyed; nearly 2,400 American lives were lost. On the evening of December 7, most Americans huddled around their radio sets to receive updates about the tragic news from the Pacific. While President Roosevelt conferred in the White House with his cabinet and met with members of Congress, the First Lady took to the airwaves. She had been scheduled to air one of her weekly broadcasts that evening as part of a six-month agreement with the Pan American Coffee Bureau. Her show was designed to highlight different aspects of the defense mobilization each week. On the night of December 7, Mrs. Roosevelt departed from her prepared remarks to address a shaken nation: "For months now the knowledge that something of this kind might happen has been hanging over our heads, and yet it seemed impossible to believe, impossible to drop the everyday things of life and feel that there was only one thing which was important—preparation to meet an enemy no matter where he struck. That is all over now, and there is no more uncertainty."

Many Cincinnatians did drop "everyday things" that night. Young men in the Queen City rushed to downtown recruiting offices of the armed forces to enlist that night. Harry Lee Dehmer, of Cheviot, and Frederick Vernon Harris, who lived in Dayton, were among the first to officially register for military service that night. After signing up, the two made their way to the Shubert Theater, accompanied by a crowd of well-wishers. When Dehmer and Harris arrived, the Andrews Sisters "adopted" them and agreed to write the two recruits when they went off to boot camp.

The next day, the president asked Congress for an official declaration of war against Imperial Japan. Just about anyone over the age of four years old remembers where they were, who they were with and what they were doing when President Roosevelt delivered his famous "day in infamy" speech before a joint session of Congress that was broadcast nationally on the radio. During his now iconic speech, in his measured cadence, Roosevelt listed all the places Japanese forces attacked in the Pacific. "Remember Pearl Harbor" soon became a rallying cry used to promote just about anything related to the war effort. When Congress cast its votes in response to the president's request for a war declaration against Japan, all the congressmen who had espoused isolationist and anti-interventionist views now affirmed the president's request. Only one lone dissenting vote was registered. Congresswoman Jeanette Rankin (Democrat, Montana), a devout pacifist, had the unique distinction of being the only person who voted against Wilson's war message in 1917 and against Roosevelt's message in 1941.

The attack on Pearl Harbor led to many important and profound changes in the lives of Cincinnatians. For one, old divisions between interventionists and isolationists quickly faded. Within a few days of the attack, J. Austin White announced that the Cincinnati AFC intended to close up shop. White declared that his group "should do all we can…to win the war as completely and as quickly as possible." The editors of the *Catholic Telegraph*, which had openly supported the AFC, published an editorial titled simply "War":

The differences of yesterday are forgotten. Personal opposition to the President and his administration ceases. Our Chief Executive now assumes the full powers of his office as commander-in-chief of all our armed forces. They are not arrayed for vengeance or destruction, but are bent on a defensive plan that will, we hope, forever deter aggressor nations from again attacking us and an offensive plan that will bring the guilty aggressor to his knees before God in repentance, suing for peace before the outraged family of nations.

The wholly unwarranted attack by Japan on the United States under conditions that seemed to postulate the most deceptive strategy of long planning can only be characterized as an act of national insanity.

Our duty is clear and simple. We must unceasingly pray that the evil spirits of war may be driven out of the souls of men everywhere and that individuals and nations may repent of their sins. We must wholeheartedly unite with our supreme commander-in-chief of the armed forces of our country to preserve the American way of life.

Likewise, Mayor Stewart, who had sympathized openly with isolationists, now proclaimed that "everyone is going to do his part to make Japanese the prevalent language in hell." Alfred Segal, who wrote under the pseudonym Cincinnatus for the *Cincinnati Post*, observed that isolationism no longer existed: "We had all been brought together under the butcher knife." Despite the terrible news from Hawaii, *Time* magazine declared that "the war came as a great relief, like a reverse earthquake, that in one terrible jerk shook everything disjointed, distorted, askew back into place. Japanese bombs had finally brought national unity to the U.S."

Cincinnati city leaders echoed this sentiment. On December 10, the city council passed a resolution affirming its support for the war:

Resolved, that we, members of City Council of Cincinnati, deem it to be fitting that we should give utterance to what we believe to be the profound unity of our people.

Our fathers and mothers offer their sons for a war that was not wanted, but that must be won.

Our workers need no lash of law upon their backs. Their loyalty will keep them at their tasks night and day.

Our citizens ask for taxes, counting it their privilege to bear their share of the common burdens.

The gloom of war is riven by the…an unconquerable purpose, and by the light of a great hope, that the victory that must come to us shall bring us also a new international order, implemented to insure [sic] the world a just and lasting peace.

Now that we have been compelled to take up arms, we pray that they shall never be laid down, until it is settled, once and for all, that arch-

murderers, who draft armies to kill and take what they covet, shall never again be tolerated on this earth.

After the attack on Pearl Harbor, editors of UC's *News Record* reversed their prewar editorial position of tolerance. Essentially, all views had been welcomed when the nation was officially neutral. Now that the United States was at war, the *News Record* would do everything in its power to support the war effort:

> *Since the beginning of school* [in 1941] *we have permitted and encouraged all students to write to the paper commenting upon the actions of the national government....Now, however, the situation has changed; and we must take cognizance of the change by closing our columns to any expressions which might be deemed contrary to the successful prosecution of the war.*

Senator Taft, it appears, represented the sole exception to this bandwagon effect. Even the news of Pearl Harbor failed to sway his distrust of and opposition to the Roosevelt administration. "Criticism in time of war," he wrote, "is essential to any kind of democratic government."

There can be little doubt that the attack on Pearl Harbor was, and continues to be, a defining moment in the course of recent American history. The die had been cast. Hitler declared war on the United States on December 11. That same day, Congress reciprocated by declaring war on the remaining Axis powers, Nazi Germany and Fascist Italy. The Roosevelt administration hoped that Americans would see this conflict as a struggle between good and evil, between fascism and totalitarianism on the one hand and democracy on the other. For the most part, Roosevelt got his wish. In the weeks after Pearl Harbor, Americans seemed more united than ever.

Yet even at that moment, one persistent division remained. Black leaders had been monitoring the ways in which the city had mobilized its resources for the defense effort. In the fall of 1940, they had expressed concern when county and city officials were slow to respond to the willingness of black men to enlist in the armed forces. Throughout 1941, many of the same black leaders had grown frustrated because they felt marginalized or excluded from opportunities to work in defense plants or to volunteer for defense-related activities. In May 1941, for example, when the Mayor's Committee on Defense formed, officials made provisions for at least one black representative, presumably Ted Berry, to be named. A few weeks after the formation of the HCNDC, as the official voice of county- and citywide defense plans, Charles Taft reminded

Morris Edwards that "we seem to have left out a [N]egro representative." One black attorney, George B. Conrad, registered complaints with Ohio governor Bricker and with New York City mayor Fiorello H. LaGuardia, the OCD head. Conrad noted bitterly: "If we are to secure national unity in this country we shall have to adopt different tactics."

Berry's law partner, William McClain, an active force for social change in Cincinnati, concurred. Earlier that fall, McClain had worked with the Cincinnati chapter of the National Association for the Advancement of Colored People (NAACP) to successfully open up downtown movie theaters to black patrons. He had organized "planned excursions [to the theaters] and vexatious litigation" throughout 1941. Cincinnati theaters had previously observed Jim Crow types of restrictions. On the heels of that victory, McClain added his voice to the chorus of people protesting the exclusion of blacks from the HCNDC. McClain proclaimed: "Because of the problems that peculiarly concern Negroes by reasons of our American traditions and culture, no Commission can truly be representative of the American people unless it has a Negro member acting in an advisory capacity and coordinating the activities of Negroes in the defense of our democracy."

During this period, the demands that Conrad, McClain and others were making could easily be misunderstood as a form of "settling," compromise or, worse, tokenism. In the context of the age of Roosevelt, it should be noted that blacks had already made substantive gains. Eleanor Roosevelt, to be sure, had a keener and more sympathetic ear in the matter of racial politics than her husband. But to his credit, President Roosevelt made efforts to appoint blacks and other minorities to positions of power. By the end of the Depression decade, Jews occupied important positions within the Roosevelt administration, including Secretary of the Treasury Henry Morgenthau and Felix Frankfurter, associate justice on the U.S. Supreme Court. It would take another thirty years before Thurgood Marshall, the first African American Supreme Court Justice, would serve in that esteemed role.

In the 1930s and 1940s, many African American appointees served in scores of federal agencies as "Negro advisors" or "Negro representatives." Mary McLeod Bethune served as the director of the Negro Division of the NYA. William Hastie, the dean of Howard University Law School, assumed additional duties as the civilian aide to Secretary of War Stimson in 1940. Individually, these public servants often felt isolated and marginalized. Collectively, their opinions and advice mattered more. They made up an unofficial body known as the "Black Cabinet" or "the Black Brains Trust." In the president, they saw a friend and ally. Once the United States entered the war, disagreements between blacks and whites over basic tenets of democracy and representative government would strain this fragile alliance.

Meanwhile, the seismic impact of Pearl Harbor still resonated across the United States. No one knew fully what to expect in the immediate aftermath of the attacks in the Pacific. Stories about panic ensuing in West Coast cities reached the Queen City. Reports about German U-boats lurking off the shores of the Atlantic and Gulf Coasts, threatening U.S. and Allied shipping, also circulated locally. Even though the likelihood of an enemy attack in a midwestern city such as Cincinnati was remote at best, city officials took what they considered were necessary precautions. C.O. Sherrill, who directed the city's skeleton force of air raid wardens, considered converting the city's unfinished subway tunnels into public bomb shelters. By that time, informed Americans had seen plenty of film footage of Londoners dutifully heading into the subway "tubes" during the German attacks on their city. A quick check by Cincinnati city officials nullified this idea because the subway tunnels, which were dug directly below street level, would offer little protection to civilians in the event of an enemy attack. The first attempts to enact citywide blackouts met with similar outcomes. Sherrill discovered that there was no easy way to extinguish the streetlights in some of the older neighborhoods that burned natural gas. He enlisted the efforts of area Boy Scouts to put out the lights individually. Sherrill also directed volunteer auxiliary policemen to guard vital bridges and public utilities plants against acts of sabotage.

Federal officials in the Queen City also took actions to calm an anxious public. In the first week of America's war, the Immigration and Naturalization Service (INS) suspended citizenship classes for 16 German aliens. Ilsa Hauer, a German immigrant who was scheduled to address her graduating class on "What Freedom Means to Me," never delivered the speech. By December 17, FBI agents had arrested and detained 29 enemy aliens (15 Germans, 12 Italians and 2 Japanese) at Fort Thomas, Kentucky. By the end of the month, local law enforcement officials in Cincinnati and Hamilton County carried out orders that required 3,500 German aliens and 1,000 Italian aliens to turn over shortwave radios, cameras and firearms to neighborhood police stations. The impact on individuals of Japanese descent was slight. The 1940 census showed that only 10 Japanese citizens and 8 aliens resided in Cincinnati. Immediately after the nation went to war, two Japanese-owned businesses, both downtown restaurants, voluntarily closed.

In the midst of so much war-induced tumult, anxiety and fear, public officials in Ohio took measures to showcase America's democratic traditions.

Before the attack on Pearl Harbor, plans were in place for all Ohio's cities to observe a weeklong, national celebration of the 150th anniversary of the Bill of Rights. December 15 had been slated as "Bill of Rights Day," and the week preceding would be known as "Bill of Rights Week." Governor Bricker went ahead with the original plans. It would be the first of many times the government used celebrations of its democratic traditions and heritage to remind Americans why they were fighting in another world war. On December 15, President Roosevelt delivered a radio address on all networks. He used the opportunity to provide both a history lesson and reiteration of war aims:

> *There is not a single Republic of this hemisphere which has not adopted in its fundamental law the basic principles of freedom of man and freedom of mind enacted in the American Bill of Rights.*
>
> *There is not a country, large or small, on this continent and in this world which has not felt the influence of that document, directly or indirectly.*
>
> *Indeed, prior to the year 1933, the essential validity of the American Bill of Rights was accepted everywhere at least in principle. Even today, with the exception of Germany, Italy, and Japan, the peoples of the whole world—in all probability four-fifths of them—support its principles, its teachings, and its glorious results.*
>
> *But in the year 1933, there came to power in Germany a political clique which did not accept the declarations of the American bill of human rights as valid: a small clique of ambitious and unscrupulous politicians whose announced and admitted platform was precisely the destruction of the rights that instrument declared. Indeed the entire program and goal of these political and moral tigers was nothing more than the overthrow, throughout the earth, of the great revolution of human liberty of which our American Bill of Rights is the mother charter.*

Former chief justice Charles Evans Hughes (1930–41) and stage and screen star Helen Hayes also spoke to listeners as part of the national radio address. Hughes delivered the bipartisan message, and Hayes provided the star power. On the same day, the Cincinnati City Council voted unanimously in favor of its own Bill of Rights resolution. Upon the suggestion of Councilman Russell Wilson, a "rising vote" was ordered and enacted:

> *The Bill of Rights…inspires us today to renew our loyalty to the principles of human equality upon which that freedom rests….This is no empty*

gesture. The times are fraught with peril to political, religious, and human liberty. Now, as when the Bill of Rights was enacted by Congress, there are those who would abrogate freedom, create tyranny through bigotry, and destroy the basic American concept that all men are created equal.

Against such attempts to overthrow or whittle away their…fundamental rights, the American people must stand firm, alike in times of peace or war. True Americans of all races and creeds, regardless of political affiliations, welcome the opportunity which the Sesqui-Centennial [sic] of the Bill of Rights affords liberty and human equality—principles upon which our nation was founded, through which alone it can endure and prosper.

The British prime minister crossed the Atlantic to confer with President Roosevelt during the first weeks of the war. Arriving in Washington, D.C., on December 22, Churchill addressed a joint session of Congress the day after Christmas. He warned that "many disappointments and surprises await us." The people of Cincinnati understood the high stakes that were evoked by this war. For the most part, they stood united in purpose, resolute and confident of ultimate victory.

Chapter 3

PULLING TOGETHER

A City United by War, 1942–44

Between late 1941 and early 1942, one could argue that very little had changed regarding Cincinnati entering the war. Men continued to enlist in the armed forces. People continued to worry and wonder about what sorts of changes the war would bring to their lives. Many people dreaded the possibility of further enemy attacks on American targets. On the other hand, much had changed. Gone was the sense of doubt and division among Americans. President Roosevelt felt unshackled and liberated to lead the country as it transitioned to a wartime footing.

Experience, as the saying goes, is a good teacher. The Great War proved to be instructive for the World War II generation. Franklin Roosevelt had served as a member of Woodrow Wilson's wartime cabinet during World War I. In January 1942, FDR, now himself in the position of a wartime commander in chief, could determine if the earlier programs from the Great War should be adopted or modified as useful templates for home front initiatives or jettisoned. One thing was for sure: the president was ready to act. Not since the "First Hundred Days" of the New Deal in 1933 had Washington, D.C., been so full of promise and action.

FDR scored his first substantive victory of the war on the diplomatic front on January 1, 1942, when he issued a proclamation entitled "A Joint Declaration of the United Nations on Cooperation for Victory." The "united nations," in this context, referred to the Allied countries fighting against the Axis powers. Representatives from twenty-four countries, including Great Britain, the Soviet Union, China, most of Nazi-occupied

Europe, the remaining members of the British Commonwealth and all of the republics of Central and South America, assembled in Washington to sign the proclamation. Each power committed "to employ its full resources, military or economic, against those members of the Tripartite Pact and its adherents with which such Government is at war." The signatory powers also agreed to not make a separate armistice or peace with the enemy at any point. Collectively, these countries wedded themselves to the goal of "complete victory" over "Hitlerism." The proclamation set the tone for the Allied war effort. This shared objective of the united nations validated earlier agreements between British and American military attachés to pursue a "Europe First" strategy. Despite the attack on Pearl Harbor and all the deep-seated emotions that were tied to that moment, any offensive actions against Imperial Japan would have to wait.

As the war progressed, the usage of the term "united nations" gave way to the "Grand Alliance." The two terms were not quite synonymous. The Grand Alliance reflected the efforts of Churchill, Roosevelt and Stalin to develop an effective and workable partnership to defeat Adolf Hitler. As of November 1941, lend-lease aid flowed to Great Britain, China and the Soviet Union. Roosevelt had already cemented a working relationship with Winston Churchill. The president knew that success in defeating the Axis powers in a two-front war would require the same level of cooperation with the Soviets. But that would take time. For Queen City residents who had favored aid to Great Britain in the early years of the conflict, lend-lease aid to the Soviets only seemed logical. Many of these people, including Russell Wilson, worked to raise money for a Russian War Relief Fund. However, for those Cincinnatians who had harbored a profound distrust of communism, such as Archbishop McNicholas, embracing the Soviets as allies would be a tall order.

The president also moved quickly on the production front. The wartime economy of 1942 led to profound changes for the nation. The first year of war proved to be a year of adjustments. As if to make good on his promise that the United States would become the great "arsenal of democracy," the president announced on January 1 that all new production of automobiles would cease indefinitely. Automobile manufacturers would soon be in the business of making airplanes, tanks and other transport vehicles necessary for war. Two weeks later, he authorized the creation of the War Production Board (WPB), headed by Donald Nelson, a vice-president on loan from Sears and Roebuck. The WPB took over the role of the Office of Production Management and supervised and coordinated the massive efforts of

During World War II, the "united nations" included every country opposed to the domination and goals of the Axis powers. While democracies naturally banded together to oppose fascism, the united nations also had to make room for nations such as the Soviet Union and China. *Courtesy of Public Library of Cincinnati and Hamilton County.*

conversion to war production. In total, more than ten thousand preexisting factories converted from peacetime to wartime production. In some cases, the process was time consuming and expensive. For other companies, the switch was quick and seamless.

Cincinnati manufacturers responded in a variety of ways. Cloplay Blinds quickly came up with a brand-new blackout curtain that could effectively darken and obscure the visibility of interior lights. This product had a special appeal in communities worried about subsequent enemy attacks in the weeks following Pearl Harbor. U.S. Playing Card modified some of its card decks. Its new wartime models included playing cards that featured silhouettes of enemy aircraft so that an informed citizenry would know how to respond in the event of an enemy attack. Baldwin Piano upended its normal manufacturing and began making wooden wings for planes that would be used to deliver mail during the war. Crosley Radio modified its line of production; it stopped making radio receivers for home use and started making radio transmitters for the military. Fashion Frocks, a local dressmaking company, began making parachutes.

One of the city's largest employers, Proctor & Gamble, made modest changes in some of its production and packaging to accommodate war shortages. Ironically, its most substantive contributions took place away from the Queen City. Immediately after the 1940 election, P&G executives created the Proctor & Gamble Defense Corporation, a new P&G subsidiary that worked closely with army ordnance officials. Proctor officials signed a contract with the War Department in which they agreed to load and package millions of ammunition shells each month. In 1941, with the help of the War Department, P&G constructed a shell-loading plant in western Tennessee. The Wolf Creek Ordnance Plant proved so successful that the War Department coaxed P&G officials to build and manage a second shell-loading plant at Aberdeen, Mississippi. Each plant met or exceeded its war production quotas and earned the coveted army-navy "E" (for excellence) Award.

While Henry Ford's mile-long Willow Run Plant, near Detroit, and the many shipyards on the Gulf and Pacific Coasts attracted the lion's share of national media attention, Cincinnati manufacturers quietly went about their business. Local businesses gained a reputation in the Midwest as an important source and supplier of component parts. The largest subcontractor in the city, of course, was the Wright Aeronautical Corporation, which supplied two types of engines for military planes. At its peak, the Lockland Plant employed more than thirty-five thousand workers.

The federal government coordinated an extensive poster campaign to maintain the morale of war workers. These posters often adorned factory walls on the shop floor. *Courtesy of Public Library of Cincinnati and Hamilton County*.

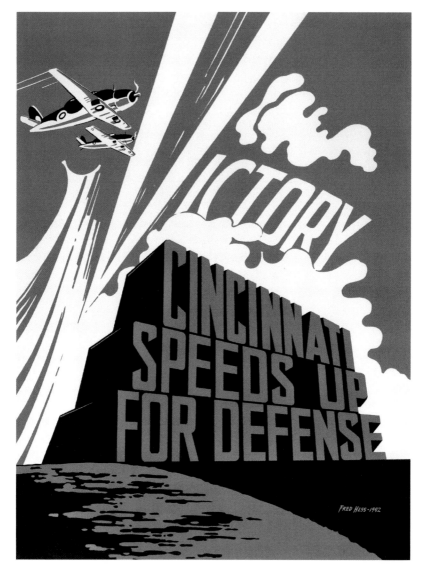

Cincinnati manufacturers responded to the federal government's call for industrial mobilization. *Courtesy of Public Library of Cincinnati and Hamilton County.*

Converting consumer goods to war production underscored other challenges facing the federal government. For a generation of workers who had suffered through the high unemployment of the Great Depression, the boom years of 1940 and 1941 were a welcome sight. Now that the nation was at war, the government had other long-term worries. The mass mobilization

While some manufacturers only needed to make slight adaptations to become vital contributors to the national defense effort, other companies, such as Baldwin Piano, had to completely overhaul its production methods. *Courtesy of Public Library of Cincinnati and Hamilton County.*

of the armed forces meant that many goods that were normally available were now funneled toward outfitting and feeding the troops. In January 1942, President Roosevelt created the Office of Price Administration (OPA) to implement and coordinate various rationing programs of consumer goods that would be in short supply.

Within a few months, rationing programs for meat, coffee, sugar, gasoline and even shoes were in place. While gas was not in short supply, motorists nonetheless found themselves facing new restrictions. The Japanese military had cut off all available access to natural rubber resources in the Far East. Through a multipronged approach, the OPA helped extend the life of tires by discouraging unnecessary or recreational driving and by imposing a maximum speed limit of thirty-five miles per hour. The OPA worked with local rationing boards. These boards distributed coupon books to each family. Formulas were created to determine how many coupons would be allotted. These formulas were based on a number of factors, including the number of family members, the level of economic need and the relative importance of the head of the family's occupation to the war effort. Cincinnatians made adjustments, large and small. Housewives learned to bake their children's birthday cakes without sugar. Schoolchildren put heavy paper bags inside their shoes to prolong the life of their soles. Deliveries from area drugstores and neighborhood groceries were suspended. Even the gas for the *Island Queen* was rationed during the summer months.

The wartime economy changed the Queen City in a multitude of ways. City leaders had to respond rapidly to vexing challenges. At first, the increase in war production led to a dramatic increase in migration. People willingly uprooted themselves, often from the rural South, in search of higher-paying jobs in Cincinnati. City leaders devised solutions to find housing for these new workers. During the earlier defense buildup, federally sponsored housing developments in the West End and in English Woods, situated on Westwood-Northern Boulevard, had filled up quickly. New housing units were eventually constructed in Norwood, Oakley and Lincoln Heights, closer to centers of war production. After the attack on Pearl Harbor, Cincinnati manufacturers suddenly faced a manpower crisis. As more and more men enlisted or received draft notices, employers realized that they would have to find and train adequate replacements from groups that had been traditionally underused or marginalized. Women and other minorities, especially African Americans, benefitted from the war-induced changes to the industrial workforce. They responded to want ads and played a major role in sustaining the arsenal of democracy.

Despite these pressing economic challenges, other concerns loomed larger in the minds of the average Cincinnatian. The first months of America's war were filled with fear. Pearl Harbor was still a fresh wound. The news of Japan's follow-up victories in the East Indies and Malaysia eroded American morale further. As commander in chief, President Roosevelt understood that the armed forces were months away from being combat ready. U.S. troops stationed in the Philippines had already retreated to the Bataan Peninsula. The surprise factor of Japan's attack on Pearl Harbor left many Americans wondering if subsequent attacks on the mainland were imminent. During January and February, in the sea lanes of the Caribbean and along the Atlantic and Gulf shorelines, German U-boats feasted on defenseless ships and liners. In February, an isolated attack by Japanese submarines off the coast of Santa Barbara confirmed the worst fears of many Americans. In Washington, D.C., officials arranged to move national treasures of art away from the nation's capital for safekeeping. The palatial Biltmore Estate, in Asheville, North Carolina, served as a temporary warehouse for the National Gallery of Art. Similarly, the Taft Museum removed some of its valuable Chinese urns and stored them in its basement for safekeeping. For the first time since the British Royal Navy wreaked havoc in Baltimore and Washington, D. C., in 1814, the nation sensed its vulnerability to other nations. The prewar rationale of the America First Committee, which stated that the nation was adequately protected by its two vast oceans, no longer seemed viable.

The president took measures to reassure the American people that they were secure from internal as well as external threats posed by the Axis powers. Since 1940, the Roosevelt administration had encouraged state and local officials to guard against the dangers of sabotage. Pearl Harbor only elevated those anxieties, especially on the West Coast. Even though no bona fide cases of sabotage had occurred on the West Coast in the weeks since Pearl Harbor, President Roosevelt signed Executive Order 9066 on February 19, 1942. This action authorized the military to take jurisdiction of all the coastal regions in California, Oregon and Washington. Moreover, the executive order allowed the military to round up anyone of Japanese descent. The fateful decision, born out of wartime anxiety and misguided assumptions about the divided loyalties of Japanese Americans, led to one of the worst cases of guilt by association or, even worse, racial profiling in our nation's history. Executive Order 9066 eventually culminated in the forced internment of more than 120,000 people of Japanese descent during the war; two-thirds of those people detained and incarcerated were American-born citizens.

Few individuals spoke out against this injustice at the time. In fact, congressman William E. Hess of Cincinnati's Second District approved of the president's actions. Hess argued that centers of war production, such as Cincinnati, were also vulnerable to acts of sabotage. Roosevelt's executive order also provided for the means to detain and intern German and Italian Americans as well as the targeted Asian population on the West Coast. Eventually, about eleven thousand German aliens in various cities across the nation were arrested and more than five thousand were interned. The war had created ethnic tensions and distrust of immigrants of German, Italian and Japanese descent. Federal laws now required enemy aliens to notify local law enforcement officials before they moved or left town. As a rule, they were prohibited from gaining employment in any war-related work.

In places, such as Cincinnati, with sizeable German American populations, it had been difficult in the 1930s to distinguish the difference between groups who were simply proud of their ethnic identities and those who sympathized with the Third Reich. One such group, the German American Citizens League, incorporated as a group in Cincinnati in 1937, loudly proclaimed that it had "zero connections" with Nazi Germany. Its raison d'être was to promote pride in "German American education, enterprise and culture and the German language." For several years, the group hosted social events at its meeting hall in Von Steuben Park in North College Hill. There, fellow German Americans could relax for a few hours, drink beer, listen to German music and get caught up on community gossip. Cognizant of its ethnic character and identity, this group of "good Germans" opted to change its name to the American Citizens League shortly after the nation entered the war.

On February 27, 1942, the American Citizens League invited Mayor Stewart and other local officials to attend its dinner dance. That Sunday afternoon, a crowd of about 250 assembled at Von Steuben Park. According to one account, a great deal of beer was consumed. After a German American spoke to the crowd about supporting the efforts of the Red Cross with donations, he introduced the guest speaker of the day, Mayor Stewart. James Garfield Stewart did not seem to mind that the position of mayor was a largely ceremonial one. He genuinely seemed to relish these types of events. Stewart began:

> *We are at war. I was one of those who hoped and prayed with all my soul that we could stay out. I used to pray to God to keep us out. But there is only one place for American citizens to be, and I know I am talking to loyal American citizens to be, and I know I am talking to loyal American citizens, and that is on the side of the American government. We have to preserve American democracy.*

The mayor offered a short history lesson about great military generals. Knowing his audience, he boasted that Frederick the Great of Prussia was "the greatest soldier Europe ever had, greater than Napoleon…the only other general I think is better is General McArthur (to which his remarks were applauded)." The mayor then spoke of the important role that Baron Von Steuben (the namesake of the park) played in training George Washington's Continental army during the Revolutionary War. Two large pictures were draped on the stage behind him: one of Washington, the other of Von Steuben. Stewart concluded his lengthy address with an expression of gratitude. He was overwhelmed by the sense of patriotism demonstrated by this German group. The mayor enthused:

> *Let us pray that the end of this war may come…Let us pray for that day to come. But let us remember that with all of our sentiments for the fatherland we are citizens of the stars and stripes and must at all times stand for the Republic. Don't ever apologize for your German ancestry or feel humiliated.*

You are entitled to just as much as anyone else. I know your loyalty, I know your fidelity. I know your faith. I salute you!

Not all German Americans made such a smooth transition. During the first two years of the war, three different facilities in Cincinnati were used to incarcerate German Americans who were arrested and detained indefinitely. Detainees were held at the Hotel Gibson, in converted space at an old post office building on Fourth Street or at the county workhouse. Five days after Mayor Stewart spoke in North College Hill, eleven German Americans were arrested by federal authorities and placed on a train at Union Terminal and transported to Sparta, Wisconsin, for long-term internment.

While the threat of possible enemy attacks to interior cities, such as Cincinnati, remained very remote in early 1942, President Roosevelt nevertheless played on those fears at a February 17 press conference, stating that the enemy "can come in and shell New York tomorrow night, under certain conditions. They can probably drop bombs on Detroit tomorrow night…under certain conditions." While his exaggerated remarks about the enemy's capabilities may have induced even more anxiety on the home front, they were intended to encourage Americans to comply with blackout regulations and other emergency drills. The Roosevelt administration hoped that enthusiasm for civilian defense measures would translate into greater support for other home front programs. One OCD staffer explained, "It is our belief that effective measures to protect the public in cases of enemy attack and effective mobilization of civilians [will] result in high civilian morale." A few months after the president's press conference, WLW radio aired a local program that reiterated the concerns about modern warfare. The announcer instructed his listeners in a folksy, but effective, geography lesson:

Do you have a map handy…the one you looked at the other night when the President was giving his fireside chat? Get it out…spread it out on the floor in front of you. See—there's Lake Erie…there's Detroit at the end of it…There's Ohio, and down at the southwestern corner, Cincinnati and Hamilton County. Distances aren't very great when you look at a world map…they aren't very great, either, as the modern giant bomb[er] flies.

The radio announcer referred to Cincinnati as "the machine tool capital" that was vital to the national war effort. One blow to Cincinnati Milling Machine, LeBlond, Wright or a dozen others "would be a knock-out blow more disastrous than Pearl Harbor…and the enemy knows it!"

Before the war began, Cincinnati had developed a reputation for being the machine tool capital of the world. *Courtesy of Public Library of Cincinnati and Hamilton County.*

The Hamilton County National Defense Council (HCNDC) responded to these perceived threats. It conducted several registration drives and ran ads in Cincinnati newspapers to fill positions for air raid wardens. The Office of Civilian Defense recommended that communities enlist sixty-three volunteers per one thousand civilians, a little more than 6 percent of the total population. Based on that ratio, Hamilton County would need around thirty-nine thousand air raid wardens. The call to action was reminiscent of the noble efforts of Cincinnati residents who erected and manned fortifications and barricades around the city during the Civil War.

The HCNDC was overwhelmed by the amount of public support to enact protective measures for the city. Public and parochial schoolteachers practiced air raid drills with students. The nuns of St. Ursula Academy, a parochial girls' school in East Walnut Hills, divided themselves into three groups: "watchers" kept a lookout for falling incendiary bombs, "sanders" kept full buckets of sand and stood ready to douse the bombs in the event of an attack and "runners" would alert civilian defense officials. The student editor of the *Woodward* [High School] *Bulldog* solemnly noted that "Cincinnati would be a favorite target for enemy planes because of its large production of machine tools so vital to the defense program." Many schools doubled as emergency field hospitals and casualty stations. Bandages and medical supplies were stored there. The HCNDC secured the use of twenty-six public and parochial schools around Hamilton County to train its legions of air raid wardens and fire watchers.

Based on the vulnerability of area industries, the city's overall contribution to the national defense effort and the likelihood of enemy attack, the OCD categorized Cincinnati as one of the nation's thirty-three most strategic cities. This designation made the city eligible to receive air raid sirens, protective equipment, medical supplies and training films. Norman P. Auburn, the dean of UC's Evening College, agreed to take charge of the HCNDC's training of air raid wardens and fire watchers. Cincinnati universities made additional contributions to the war effort. Dr. Leon Goldman, assistant professor of dermatology, conducted a course for physicians who attended from several neighboring states to learn about the harmful effects of chemical warfare on civilian populations. Xavier University assisted the HCNDC by playing host to the commencement ceremonies of more than six thousand air raid wardens.

HCNDC officials fretted over their ability to train enough air raid wardens in civilian defense procedures in densely populated downtown

Civil defense officials erected an outdoor display near Fountain Square in March 1942 to heighten interest in air raid precautions. *Courtesy of American Jewish Archives.*

Norman Auburn, dean of the College of Evening Education at the University of Cincinnati, volunteered to offer training for air raid wardens and other civilian defense personnel in 1942. *Courtesy of University of Cincinnati Archives.*

neighborhoods as well as the outlying suburbs. One civilian defense official in Cincinnati admitted frankly that he had "no idea how far progress has gone in congested areas of the city, where fire…could sweep and cover many blocks, while trouble in the suburbs would be unlikely to spread." Several

Cincinnati zoo officials assured residents of surrounding neighborhoods that in the event of an emergency "the Zoo force is prepared to destroy animals that would be a menace if they should get loose." *Courtesy of Public Library of Cincinnati and Hamilton County.*

suburban communities, such as Wyoming, Sharonville and Cheviot, had devoted significant resources toward implementing air raid precautions in their communities. The same was not always true in the poorer and more densely populated parts of the inner city. Moreover, the HCNDC had been slow to welcome and include blacks, who made up a significant percentage of residents in those crucial downtown neighborhoods, among those being recruited to protect the city.

The fact that the HCNDC had attracted few blacks to its ranks in the early months of 1942 reflected a broader concern among wartime officials in Washington, D.C., and Cincinnati about "Negro morale." Wartime activism for blacks in the 1940s was, in many respects, defined by double-entendres. When Roosevelt signed Executive Order 8802 in May 1941, creating the Fair Employment Practices Committee to end the practice of racial discrimination in defense plants, optimistic blacks called the action a "second Reconstruction." Distrustful whites, who resented the president's actions, used the same words to express their contempt for this policy, conjuring up unhappy memories of an oppressive government forcing its will on the defeated Confederate states. In 1942, the same duality existed over the use of the term "Negro morale." In the aftermath of Pearl Harbor, many blacks—buoyed by the president's egalitarian and democratic rhetoric—looked hopefully for signs that any discussions about "Negro morale" would lead to concrete policies for enhancing their ability to support the war effort.

Many blacks assumed that any discussions about morale would lead to greater opportunities of full-fledged participation in war-related activities.

The Roosevelt administration assumed, on the other hand, that the lingering effect of Pearl Harbor would unite all Americans behind the war effort "regardless of race, creed, or color." Many federal officials failed to take into account that prewar customs of racial discrimination limited or curbed blacks' ability to support the war. A gulf existed between the wartime expectations of whites and blacks in this conversation about black morale. One government study in early 1942 went so far as to suggest that low rates of black participation reflected a possible allegiance toward the Japanese. Blacks simply wanted the chance to participate equally, whether in uniform, in home front tasks or in the workplace.

When those chances were slow to materialize and old patterns of discrimination remained, emboldened black leaders countered with a new set of demands. In February 1942, the editors of the *Pittsburgh Courier*, an influential black weekly, coined the expression "Double Victory." This elegant concept allowed blacks to proclaim support for the larger aims of the war effort by defending democracy abroad. At the same time, it allowed blacks to continue to work for social and economic justice at home. "Double Victory" offered them a seemingly obvious solution in which they could patriotically support the war and remain true to their concerns about improving the lot of their group. Ted Berry's brief stint in Washington, D.C., illustrates just how far apart whites and blacks were on the issues of black participation and black morale.

Shortly after the attack on Pearl Harbor, Berry resigned his position of assistant prosecutor of Hamilton County and offered his services to the Office of Facts and Figures, the federal government's principal morale agency at that time. Berry came to Washington armed with idealistic notions about how to more accurately represent the efforts of blacks "doing their bit." Berry's tenure ended abruptly in April 1942. He resigned in disgust when he made the startling discovery that government documentary filmmakers allowed for the inclusion of only 1 "black" image per every 150 "nonblack" images in any given film. When he brought this to the attention of his immediate superior, a white southern businessman who owned a chain of black theaters, his complaint went nowhere. The "higher ups" in the agency defended the policy as appropriate. Even after his resignation, Berry continued to send federal officials suggestions on ways to develop strategies to better include blacks in all phases of the war effort. When those suggestions fell on deaf ears, Berry returned to

Cincinnati, discouraged but still determined to elicit changes to improve the plight of black Americans.

Berry's short-lived experience working for the federal government cast a spotlight on a larger and troubling pattern of persistent race bias that lingered on the home front. Having witnessed such intransigent attitudes about race in the nation's capital, Berry gained insights into the problems blacks continued to face in the Queen City. When OCD officials observed that black participation in civilian defense classes in Cincinnati was lower than the overall white turnout, some federal and state officials jumped to the conclusion that Cincinnati's blacks were being less than patriotic. William Lovelace, a black probate official in Hamilton County, had been appointed as the Negro representative to the HCNDC. In April 1942, Lovelace organized a "mammoth mass meeting" to encourage greater participation by area blacks in civilian defense. Lovelace rented out the Taft Auditorium and invited more than one hundred different black religious, social, civic and fraternal organizations to participate. He also ran a full-page ad in the *Cincinnati Independent*, a black weekly, to generate interest for the meeting. An estimated 2,300 people crowded into the Taft for the April 10 meeting. A detachment of black soldiers from Fort Knox, Kentucky, attended the event along with a military band. The WPA Symphony kicked off the festivities with its rendition of "The Star Spangled Banner." Lovelace, who served as the master of ceremonies, introduced a long list of impressive speakers for the event. Among them was Jesse Locker, a black Republican member of the Cincinnati City Council; Mayor Stewart; Charles V. Carr, the race relations advisor in the OCD regional office in Cleveland; Governor Bricker; and J. Harvey Kearns, the executive secretary of the Negro Division of the Cincinnati Community Chest. The meeting had the potential, as expressed by the *Times-Star*, to emphasize "a need for greater integration of Negroes in the total program of civilian protection." After Governor Bricker, Mayor Stewart and Harry Gilligan, the commander of Cincinnati's air raid wardens, addressed the crowd, Charles Carr followed suit. His views came closest to reflecting the official policy in wartime Washington. Total war demanded total support of the American people. Wartime unity was the paramount goal. According to the *Enquirer*, Carr "told the assembly that Negroes had been deprived of their rights many times. He urged that this should not prevent the Negro Race from doing its full duty in the present emergency…their failure would be used against them after the war."

Expressions about wartime unity had never seemed so important as they did in the spring of 1942. Likewise, civil defense planning had taken on an added sense of urgency. Ever since the attack on Pearl Harbor, there had been almost no good news to report from the Pacific. Imperial Japanese forces had seized the offensive and appeared unstoppable. U.S. troops hunkered down in the Philippines. After a three-month siege, General Douglas McArthur received orders to withdraw from the region. On April 9, the combined U.S.-Filipino forces surrendered to the Japanese. Unfortunately, the news became even bleaker when Japanese captors forced POWs to endure a lengthy and brutal march. During the so-called Bataan Death March, what would later be classified as a war crime, many prisoners who were too weak to walk were killed or left for dead along the way.

Later that same month, the first hint of positive news from the Pacific was shared with the home front. On April 18, Americans learned of the heroics of Lieutenant Colonel James "Jimmy" Doolittle, who led a squadron of sixteen B-25 bombers on a daring daylight raid over Tokyo. The Doolittle Raid, designed to strike terror in the hearts of the Japanese home front and to restore a sense of hope and optimism among the American people, succeeded on both fronts. While the mission did little actual damage to its intended targets, it renewed a sense of hope and determination to keep fighting. UC president Raymond Walters wrote in his diary on April 18: "If the report is true…the effect throughout the Orient will be marked. The bombing of Japan, with the power it indicates and the future it suggests, will do much to restore American prestige."

While Cincinnatians struggled to keep abreast of the war-related news in Asia and North Africa, at times, the war elbowed its way right into the city. For nearly a month in the late spring of 1942, more than six hundred Axis diplomats, consular officials and their families lodged in the top four floors of the Hotel Gibson. This surreal internment was part of a larger international exchange between Axis diplomats still residing in Allied nations in the Western Hemisphere and American and Latin American diplomatic personnel who shared a similar plight in Axis-controlled Europe. Hotel staff extended every possible courtesy to the enemy aliens. The Hotel Gibson brought hair stylists and barbers on site to service its guests. Foods that had seemingly been in short supply in downtown restaurants, such as coffee, bacon and fruit juices, were readily available to the Axis guests. Stenographers who were fluent in German were summoned to the hotel to write letters for some of the detainees. During the the detention at the Hotel Gibson, one female Japanese envoy who was pregnant was taken to Jewish Hospital, where she gave birth to her baby. When the enemy aliens finally departed the city, one female German detainee expressed her sincere gratitude to the Queen City for her treatment: "Is it like this everywhere in the United States? We have been treated grand. It is a shame, this war." The detainees were transported to Union Terminal and left the city via rail to New York City. From there, they sailed aboard the *Drottingholm* on their way to Lisbon, Portugal.

Of course, not all images of the enemy were as benign as these Axis envoys that passed through Cincinnati. In June 1942, federal officials uncovered a German plot that sounded too fantastic to be true. As the story unfolded, it sounded like something generated by pulp-fiction novelists or Hollywood scriptwriters. In unexpected ways, the plot involved Cincinnati and brought the potential horrors of war closer to home.

In late May, two four-man crews of German soldiers, recruited and trained in Germany in the art of sabotage, set sail from Lorient, France. On June 13, the first group landed near Long Island, New York. Four days later, the second group arrived just south of Jacksonville, Florida, and prepared to travel by train to Cincinnati. The original plan called for all eight men to meet in Cincinnati on July 4. By that point, the leader of the Long Island group had panicked and ultimately turned himself in to the FBI in New York City before any acts of sabotage had been committed. Within a matter of days, all eight would-be saboteurs had been arrested by the FBI. The Roosevelt administration wasted no time trying the men in front of military tribunals.

During the course of their interrogation, FBI officials learned that one of the teams of German commandos had been given orders to blow up an important hydroelectric plant near Niagara Falls as well as locks along the Ohio River between Pittsburgh and Louisville. The second team had been assigned the task of placing bombs in Jew-owned department stores and in train stations to induce mass panic. Happily, none of these dreadful acts were carried out. At the conclusion of the military tribunal, six of the Germans were sentenced to death; the sentence was carried out that August. Two others received lengthy prison terms.

During their investigation, federal officials also learned that the man who recruited and trained the eight commandos, Lieutenant Walter Kappe, had emigrated from Germany to the United States in 1925. From 1931 until 1937, Kappe lived in Cincinnati and wrote a society column about "parties given by clubs, theatre performances and subjects pertaining to literature" for Cincinnati's *Freie Press*. Long suspected of being pro-Nazi, Kappe had been under FBI surveillance since the mid-1930s. He lost his job when he attempted to voice pro-Nazi views. He returned home to Germany and took his place in the Abwehr, the military intelligence branch of the Nazi Party.

Nazi saboteurs had trained to blow up important locks on the Ohio River near Cincinnati. Their capture by FBI agents in June 1942 fortunately thwarted any such attempts. *Courtesy of Kenton County Library.*

Given Kappe's familiarity with U.S. geography, language and American customs, he was tasked with finding recruits for the sabotage mission. Federal officials worried that additional missions had been planned. Assuming that Kappe was in the United States to coordinate those plans, a countrywide manhunt ensued. The headline story for the *Cincinnati Post* on July 25, 1942, reflected the palpable anxieties of administration officials: "Ex-Cincinnatian Hunted As Spy." The manhunt failed to yield any positive results. Kappe was never captured. Given the spectacular failure and embarrassment of this operation, Hitler never attempted a follow-up mission against the United States home front.

By June 1942, events halfway around the world had taken a marked turn for the better. The Battle of Midway, a stunning Allied victory, marked the beginning of the U.S. counteroffensive in the Pacific theater. Reports from Midway marked the first good news for the Allies since the Doolittle Raid in April. Important Allied victories in North Africa soon followed.

Ironically, just as the Queen City began to train adequate numbers of air raid wardens and other personnel to protect its communities, the danger of enemy air raids—which had seemed so vital a few months earlier— diminished. But the improved military conditions did not weaken the Americans' dedication and resolve to the war effort. As a result, the federal civilian defense authorities maintained their commitment to the readiness of community-based volunteers. Whenever wartime shortages and priorities permitted, the OCD allocated firefighting equipment to "target areas," including Cincinnati.

Local civilian defense officials did their part by trying to maximize the authenticity of the city's air raid drills. In July, C.O. Sherrill and Harry Gilligan, a local funeral director and volunteer "commander" of Cincinnati's air raid wardens, gathered on a dark hillside in Fairmount, overlooking the Mill Creek, to observe the first citywide blackout. The thrilled onlookers watched as the city's skyline went completely dark for the first time. That November, just after civilian defense officials installed large "victory sirens" on the rooftops of the tallest downtown buildings, plans were announced for the most elaborate drill yet. Planes were scheduled to fly over the city and drop "simulated bombs," small cardboard cylinders with red crepe paper streamers. Each "bomb" contained a message, rolled up inside the cylinder, describing its destructive capability:

> *I AM A BOMB*
> *My Purpose is to Destroy Your home, Your store,*
> *Your building, Your Factory.*
> *I have been sent to maim and kill YOU, YOUR*
> *FAMILY, YOUR FRIENDS, YOUR NEIGHBORS.*
> *I am 21 inches long, I weigh 5 pounds. I am*
> *both incendiary and explosive.*
> *Report ME.*
> *Imagine the damage I'll do if not reported.*
> *Look where I've landed. Imagine the damage*
> *I would do.*
> *Report ME.*

The cylinders were numbered so they could easily be reported to defense officials. Unfortunately, inclement weather on the day of the drill grounded all air traffic. Nevertheless, the bombs still "fell." Determined HCNDC staffers traveled by automobile around the city and tossed the cylinders out of car windows.

Even though American cities were never bombed as anticipated, civilian defense volunteers applied their training to other home front problems. Nurses' aides, who had been trained by the Red Cross to work in emergency field hospitals in the aftermath of an enemy attack, assisted hospital personnel during natural disasters and accidents. In early January 1943, civilian defense workers in Pennsylvania, West Virginia and Ohio assisted the Red Cross in evacuating more than thirty-two thousand people from flooded areas of the Ohio River Valley. The *Cincinnati Enquirer* praised the effort: "Perhaps part of this ready and efficient cooperation was the result of know-how, of experience gained in the catastrophe of half a decade ago. But part of it stemmed from the greater sense of civic responsibilities that has grown out of the program of civilian defense and kindred wartime activities."

News of victories in the Pacific and North Africa allowed those on the home front to worry less about defending their factories and neighborhoods. Many of those same people who volunteered to serve as air raid wardens and fire watchers could now redirect their efforts. No longer in a defensive posture, the American people looked for substantive ways in which they could "do their bit." The home front population supported the war effort in a wide variety of ways. Some support was voluntary. Some efforts were mandated by federal agencies in Washington; they were designed to appeal to the strong sense of patriotism and duty of the average citizen.

Most popular home front campaigns were tied either directly or indirectly to the demands of the wartime economy. The shift to war production created shortages of raw materials. Officials in Washington encouraged city and state officials to develop salvage programs. Local defense councils mobilized communities to participate in campaigns for raw materials such as waste paper, brass, rubber and copper. More than 95 percent of U.S. cities with populations greater than twenty-five thousand had organized salvage committees as a part of their civilian defense organizations. It is difficult to determine just how much volunteer scrap drives actually contributed to the war effort. Nevertheless, some cities went to extraordinary lengths to obtain scarce materials.

The first salvage drive in Cincinnati occurred five months before America's entry into the war. Unfortunately, city officials in July 1941 failed to master the logistics involved in coordinating such an event from start to finish. After tons of scrap aluminum were collected in a giant bin near the federal building on Fountain Square, no plan was in place to remove it. The scrap remained for weeks, leaving donors with the impression that their coffee pots and cooking pans would never be processed and converted into anything useful. Such failures and inconsistencies had been addressed by the spring of 1942. Salvage drives became common expressions of a determined and patriotic citizenry to help the war effort. In Cincinnati and Hamilton County, the HCNDC coordinated neighborhood drives for scarce items. Harold W. Nichols, president of the Fox Paper Company in Lockland, served as the chair of the Waste Materials Conservation Committee.

Cincinnatians willingly "got in the scrap" by participating in salvage drives for scrap metal, rubber, waste paper and other scarce materials to assist the war effort. *Courtesy of Public Library of Cincinnati and Hamilton County.*

Nichols devised creative ways to coax Cincinnatians of all ages to participate in these vital home front campaigns. One of the earliest efforts, "a scrap drive matinee," occurred in February 1942. Youngsters who donated items to a neighborhood scrap drive were granted "free" admission to the weekly double feature at an area movie theater. Nichols also took advantage of the friendly rivalry that existed between the student bodies at Xavier University and the University of Cincinnati to coordinate a scrap drive competition. At stake were bragging rights for the student body that collected the most scrap. Xavier came up with the winning strategy. These zealous students dedicated an entire practice football field as a drop-off center for donated golf clubs, furnaces and even auto parts. The Xavier students handily beat their crosstown rivals. The victors collected six tons more than their counterparts and bought war bonds with the proceeds they earned from the competition. Nichols repeatedly enlisted the help of local Boy Scout troops to participate in door-to-door campaigns. He also arranged for city officials to place five hundred barrels painted red, white and blue around the city. The barrels served as drop-off centers for scrap donations. Toward the end of the war, in 1944, the number of receptacles for scrap had grown to more than two thousand barrels placed in neighborhoods all over the city.

Under Nichols's energetic leadership, the Queen City had developed a national reputation as a trailblazer in the area of wartime salvage. In June, he received a special citation from OCD officials in Washington, D.C., which noted that Cincinnati had collected more scrap than any other major city in the United States. His "Cincinnati Plan" served as a model for hundreds of other cities that were developing salvage committees. Home front campaigns could only be successful if its participants felt their actions were tied in some way to the larger war effort. A simple reminder of that connection came from E.J. Boos, a columnist for an in-house newsletter for the Cincinnati Street Railway Car Company. Boos told readers in May 1942 that salvage drives did not exist to keep the cost of business down but to aid soldiers on the fighting fronts. Boos continued: "If you miss that metal clip that used to hold lead pencil erasers, reflect that the metal saved would make about 130,000,000 cartridge cases for our soldiers."

In Nichols's eyes nothing was off limits. Abandoned streetcar rails were torn up and donated for scrap. At one point during the war, Nichols wrote to Councilman Charles Taft, asking for permission to scrap an abandoned water pump that the city owned: "I hardly need to dwell upon the vital necessity for scrap iron and metals...[this station] contains many hundred tons of scrap iron badly needed for winning the war." The Paramount

Woodward High School agreed to tear down its cast-iron fence that surrounded its campus during a wartime salvage drive. *Courtesy of Public Library of Cincinnati and Hamilton County.*

Theater on Gilbert Avenue donated its giant steel tower, well known as a local landmark at Peebles Corner in Walnut Hills. Cheviot willingly gave the cast-iron bell from its town hall building. Area junkyards offered up abandoned automobiles and farm machinery.

The *Times-Star* had speculated earlier in the war whether Civil War–era cannon at local American Legion and VFW halls might not make suitable donations. The editors noted that these cannon may be "tarnished and weather-beaten but still a worthwhile investment as scrap metal for national defense…[they] might be fashioned into something usable against Herr Hitler and his Axis playmates." By the summer of 1942, the federal government was exploring the possibility of collecting large inventories of historic cannon and similar armaments to scrap for the current military purposes. The government started searching old navy yards and army camps for outdated guns and cannons. At an August 7 press conference, President Roosevelt was asked what guidelines existed for states and cities to donate Civil War cannon and statues for scrap purposes. The president joked that some statues (presumably those of Republicans) would look better if they were melted into scrap. Amid the banter with the reporters, FDR supported the idea of scrapping iron cannon: "I am inclined to think that it wouldn't be a bad idea to get some kind of approval or authorization by Congress which would tell communities that have these cannon out on the village green that after the war is all over we will replace them with something more modern… that has a modern history in the winning of th[is] war."

The discussion about cannon and statuary resonated with salvage officials in Cincinnati. Some city officials suggested that the statue of the *Capitoline Wolf*, in Eden Park, be donated to the cause. The City of Cincinnati had received this bronze statue in 1931 from Italian dictator Benito Mussolini as part of a goodwill, cultural exchange in a sister city program. The *Capitoline Wolf* depicted the story of Romulus and Remus, the twin brothers who figured prominently in the creation story of ancient Rome. With tensions running high against the Axis powers in 1942, the sacrifice of this Roman statue seemed logical, if not inevitable. Somehow, cooler heads prevailed, and the statue remained. Silently, Italian Americans in Cincinnati breathed a sigh of relief.

By the fall of 1942, salvage drives had become commonplace events in Cincinnati neighborhoods. People of all ages participated. The editors of the University of Cincinnati *News Record* reminded their readers how important

The statue of the *Capitoline Wolf* had become a fixture at Eden Park since the early 1930s. Happily, it escaped the efforts of overzealous citizens to melt it down for scrap during the war. *Courtesy of Cincinnati Parks Board.*

these efforts were to the war effort: "We are forging our scrap iron, steel, tin, rubber, into a Hari-Kari sword for the Mikado; a keen-edged rapier that will eventually be thrust into the heart of the Nazi regime. Il Duce will feel its sting through the disintegration of his Axis brothers."

War bond campaigns were staged almost as frequently as salvage drives. In an era dominated by Keynesian theories of economics, the federal government projected that deficit spending and higher taxes would pay for about two-thirds of the war costs. The remainder would have to be borne by the people. The precedent for war bonds had been made in the Great War. During that brief but momentous conflict, civilians purchased interest-bearing financial notes from the government called Liberty Bonds. The U.S. Treasury Department revived that practice during 1940–41, selling defense stamps and bonds. In 1942, Roosevelt's secretary of the treasury, Henry Morgenthau Jr., lobbied for a more aggressive campaign. He felt that the average wage earner needed to purchase war bonds early and often. By doing so, Americans could become stakeholders in the larger war effort, engaged in a form of "participatory democracy." In addition to the patriotic connotations, war bond purchases would help curb runaway inflation by siphoning disposable income out of the marketplace. An "E" series war bond sold for $18.75. After ten years, it matured to $25.00. At the national level, more than eighty-five million Americans purchased a whopping $135 billion in war bonds during the course of seven different national campaigns.

Volunteers who organized these campaigns at the state and local levels were granted nearly full autonomy regarding the methods they employed to generate interest in war bond sales. John J. Rowe, the president of Fifth-Third Bank, chaired the Hamilton County War Savings Committee. Rowe worked with the HCNDC to coordinate war bond drives in the Queen City. Volunteers known as "bondadiers" went door to door, canvassing for purchases. Schools also cooperated with the bond drives. Schoolchildren contributed smaller donations each Tuesday and Thursday—nickels and dimes—toward the purchase of defense stamps. Once enough stamps were purchased, they were redeemed for an actual war bond.

In May 1942, the War Savings Committee constructed a war bond pier on Fountain Square with donated construction materials and "free labor" provided by inmates from the city's workhouse. The war bond pier became the focal point of many patriotic events staged on or near Fountain Square to keep the attention of the home front riveted on the war. The War Savings Committee sponsored concerts, parades and other patriotic events in this public space to promote war bond sales. In July, a wooden replica of a

On nearly any given week, Fountain Square hummed with war bond drives, blood drives and other war-related activities. Military cadets from Xavier University assembled downtown in 1942 for a patriotic pageant. *Courtesy of Xavier University Archives.*

battleship called the USS *Victory* was built and placed on Fountain Square to remind citizens (as if they needed reminding) that the nation was still at war and needed their support. The battleship functioned as a naval recruiting office and a kiosk for war bond purchases.

Similar to the campaigns to raise awareness of civilian defense, war bond rallies were segregated affairs. Nationally, composer Irving Berlin gave singer Kate Smith the freedom to sing his popular anthem, "God Bless America," at war bond rallies. Her performances led to more than $600 million in war bond sales. Simultaneously, the Treasury Department obtained permission from the U.S. Army for heavyweight boxer Joe Louis (aka the "Brown Bomber") to make appearances at black war bond rallies. This pattern of segregation persisted in Cincinnati as well. In June 1942, Hollywood actress Marlena Dietrich made a scheduled appearance in the Queen City on behalf of the Treasury Department to sell war bonds. In October, Etta Moten, the well-known African American actress and singer who starred in George Gershwin's *Porgy and Bess* on Broadway, came to Cincinnati. Between her scheduled performances at the Taft Theater, she also encouraged Cincinnati blacks to buy bonds.

Treasury secretary Morgenthau called the war bond campaigns "the greatest sales operation in history." This claim was neither idle boast nor hyperbole. Cincinnatians could not escape the appeals that were targeted at them on a daily basis. Characters on nationally syndicated radio shows, such as *Fibber McGee and Molly*, made overt pleas to listeners to buy bonds. Cartoon characters like Bugs Bunny reminded passive moviegoers of their patriotic duty. A massive advertising campaign in Cincinnati generated posters and ads on streetcars. In June 1942, the War Savings Committee dropped leaflets over the city, via airplane, urging Cincinnatians to devote 10 percent of their weekly paychecks to the purchase of war bonds. When the majority of workers at any given worksite earmarked 10 percent of their paychecks toward the purchase of war bonds, that company was eligible to fly a U.S. Treasury Minuteman Flag on its work premises. Before the eight bond drives concluded, more than three hundred Cincinnati businesses qualified for this coveted award.

Wherever Cincinnatians went around town, whatever activity they engaged in, they were reminded of all the ways that everyday life had changed. During its spring 1942 term, the University of Cincinnati's Evening College replaced two of its traditional political science courses concerning state and local politics with courses entitled "Modern Democracy: Its Roots and Fundamentals" and "The Politics of Totalitarianism." For the first time in school history, owing to the impact of the military draft on college campuses, women occupied the prestigious positions of editor and business manager for the *News Record*. The war yielded an unexpected bonus for operagoers. The summer opera series at the zoo featured several top

European performers who were unable to perform in their home countries due to the war. Wartime reminders even showed up at Crosley Field. During the Reds' 1942 season, patriotic signs appeared on the left field. Some of the signs offered the familiar refrain to "Remember Pearl Harbor." Others reminded fans to purchase war bonds and to "avoid waste." The Reds also announced that all balls hit into the stands would be donated to the men in uniform for recreational activities.

By the fall of 1942, Cincinnatians had made many important adjustments to the war. Nearly every action by families—how and when they shopped, where they worked, how they traveled around town—everything now seemed to be shaped by the war. Whether the average Cincinnatian knew it or not, the local defense council had played a vital role in coordinating a wide range of war-related activities on the home front.

In order to maintain those levels of support, the Office of Civilian Defense came up with a campaign in September 1942 called the "V[ictory] Home Campaign." Air raid wardens canvassed their neighborhoods and asked homeowners if they participated in scrap drives, conserved clothing and food and other vital materials, purchased war bonds, refused to spread Axis rumors and (of course) obeyed instructions from air raid wardens. The warden conducted no exacting interviews, relying instead on the word of the respondents. Affirmative responses entitled worthy families to receive a "V-Home" sticker in the front windows of their houses. Cincinnati families proudly displayed these decals through the remainder of the war.

Overall, the Roosevelt administration seemed satisfied with the new direction the country had taken during its first year of war. The overall willingness of the American people to deal with shortages and to endure sacrifices of all sorts eased the administration's concerns about home front morale and wartime unity. Nearly ten months after Japan attacked Pearl Harbor, President Franklin D. Roosevelt went on a cross-country tour of military training facilities, war plants and war-impacted communities to evaluate the home front's performance. Returning to Washington in mid-October, FDR noted confidently in a fireside chat: "This nation of 130,000,000 free men, women, and children is becoming one great fighting force. Some of us are soldiers or sailors, some of us are civilians... each of us is playing an honorable part in the great struggle to save our democratic civilization."

The president also paid tribute to the more than ten million people who had volunteered: "They are displaying unselfish devotion in the patient performance of their tiresome and always anonymous tasks. In doing this important neighborly work they are helping to fortify our national unity and our real understanding of the fact that we are all involved in this war."

Morale had been a paramount concern of officials in Washington, D.C., since the start of the defense mobilization in 1940. In June 1942, Roosevelt authorized the creation of the Office of War Information (OWI), which replaced the Office of Facts and Figures. The OWI was tasked with creating original content for war-related campaigns for salvage efforts, war bond sales, car pool drives to conserve fuel and the like. OWI staffers also had to supervise and, to a degree, censor prepared content for newspaper and magazine articles and movie and radio scripts as well as prepare speeches by public officials and posters. In the world we inhabit today—the so-called information age—it is hard to fathom just how inundated the home front had become with wartime propaganda. Daily news was regulated and sanitized to the point that one historian referred to this era as America's "censored war."

One of the unresolved issues for the federal government concerned African Americans. The mass mobilization of men for the armed forces coupled with the mobilization of the industrial workforce created a climate of optimism among blacks that they would soon gain some measures of social and economic equality. When those anticipated changes failed to keep pace with the expectations of blacks, trouble ensued. In June 1943, a full-fledged race riot erupted in Detroit, Michigan, a little more than 250 miles away from the Queen City. As one of the leading centers of war production, Detroit had experienced even more growth and resultant strain on its infrastructure than Cincinnati. Blacks and whites had migrated to Detroit in record numbers since 1941. They competed fiercely for jobs and housing. Tensions finally boiled over in June 1943. Unsubstantiated rumors of violence by white mobs directed against innocent blacks triggered a three-day orgy of violence between groups of whites and blacks in Detroit. Order was restored only when federal troops were called in. The riot led to thirty-four deaths and more than four hundred reported injuries, as well as about $2 million in property damage from looting and arson. That dollar amount would equal nearly $28 million in 2014.

The Detroit race riot sent shock waves throughout the Midwest. The awful realization that "it could happen here" spurred Cincinnatians to react quickly. Community leaders pressed Mayor Stewart to form a committee that could address and alleviate some of the city's chronic racial and ethnic issues. Stewart appointed a cross section of prominent Queen City residents—including Ted Berry; Monsignor Marcellus Wager of the Archdiocese of Cincinnati; Reverend Nelson Burroughs, the rector at Christ Church; and Robert Segal, of the Jewish Community Relations Committee—to serve on the Mayor's Friendly Relations

Committee (MFRC). One commentator noted that "the original concept of [M]FRC as chiefly intended to 'prevent riots' has grown into a wiser, wider vision of its long term function to build friendly understanding and mutual respect among citizens of every creed, color and condition."

The MFRC recognized that war-induced changes threatened to create a pressure cooker environment in most major U.S. cities, Cincinnati included, when it came to the competition over war jobs, limited housing and poor or insufficient recreational and health services and facilities. MFRC members felt their city had many viable networks of civic and church groups that could promote and foster the group's vision of racial and ethnic harmony. They suggested that civilian defense officials—namely, air raid wardens and "block captains" who helped facilitate civilian war services to neighborhoods— were ideally positioned to deliver the message of the mayor's committee. The MFRC also worked through church and civic organizations to calm racial and ethnic tensions. During the tumultuous summer of 1943, race riots occurred with alarming frequency in several major cities and near or on military bases. Happily, the Queen City was spared such a fate.

Many of the same people who worked to calm racial and religious tensions in Cincinnati also helped another ethnic group—Japanese Americans transitioning from internment camps—to new homes and jobs in the Queen City. Beginning in May 1943, the War Relocation Authority (WRA), the federal agency that had supervised the mass incarceration of Japanese Americans since February 1942, relaxed many of its own wartime policies concerning internment. Internees were now encouraged to find gainful employment outside the camps. The Pacific Coast, home to most Japanese Americans, was still off limits. The WRA initiative required internees to resettle in communities east of the Mississippi River and in relatively small numbers. By avoiding a mass migration or influx of Japanese Americans toward any one city or locale, WRA officials felt that most negative responses to its resettlement efforts could be minimized.

By the summer of 1943, Cincinnati emerged as a popular destination for Japanese American internees who wanted to avoid larger midwestern cities like Chicago or Cleveland. The strategy worked. More than seven hundred internees made their way out of the various camps to resettle in Cincinnati. The American Friends Service Committee, the social justice arm of the Quakers, took a lead role in helping Japanese Americans make the transition to life outside the camps. Raymond Booth, a Quaker minister from California, quit his job and moved to Cincinnati to become the WRA representative there. Booth and his wife, Gracia, became the first directors of

Reverend Nelson Burroughs, rector of Christ Cathedral, helped Japanese American internees make a smooth transition to life in wartime Cincinnati. *Courtesy of the Christ Church Cathedral Archives.*

a hostel for internees, located on Winslow Avenue in Walnut Hills. A second hostel, operated by the Episcopal Church, opened on the same street a few months later. The Booths worked with Protestant, Catholic and Jewish leaders to form the Cincinnati Citizens Committee for the Resettlement of Japanese Americans. Earlier in the war, Cincinnatians had participated in salvage drives that were designed to "slap the Jap." By 1943, thousands of moviegoers had been subjected to the negative portrayals of Japanese saboteurs in films such as *Tokyo, U.S.A.* and of the ruthless and villainous soldiers in combat films like *Bataan* and *The Purple Heart.* Moreover, Cincinnatians were not immune to stories of wartime atrocities committed by Imperial Japanese troops in the Pacific. It was up to the Booths to combat these negative stereotypes. One tactic they employed was to show a government documentary entitled *Challenge to Democracy* to various civic groups. The film included highlights of Japanese American soldiers fighting the Axis forces. In April 1943, the *Cincinnati Times-Star* voiced its support for the resettlement effort: "It would

One WRA pamphlet touted the appeal of the Queen City's family values to induce internees to come to Cincinnati. It referred to Cincinnati as "a city of families." *Courtesy of Public Library of Cincinnati and Hamilton County.*

be in the American tradition to make the Nisei [most of the internees were second-generation Japanese Americans] of proved loyalty feel at home here. Would it not be rather dumb in a time of manpower scarcity…to leave that reservoir of skill and industry untapped[?]"

Kate and Arthur Brinton replaced the Booths as hostel directors in June 1943. Arthur Brinton had been classified as a conscientious objector to the war. Reverend John Yamazaki, an Episcopal minister with extensive experience working with Japanese Americans in Los Angeles before the war, was assigned to manage the other hostel. Another committee member, Claude Courter, superintendent of the city's public schools, committed to help Japanese American schoolchildren feel welcome in their new classrooms.

The hostels provided safe havens for the new arrivals. Camp officials gave internees enough money to travel by train to the destination of their choosing. Cincinnati's new hostel directors met new internees at Union Terminal. They allowed the newcomers to spend a few nights at the hostel and ultimately helped them to secure more permanent housing and employment. Some internees complained about isolated incidents of racism. Benny Okura, a young internee who arrived from a camp in Arkansas, remembered being denied admission to the Albee Theater and the Mills Restaurant downtown. On the other hand, Okura warmly recalled the willingness of Jewish landlords in Avondale to rent apartments to Japanese American families. For the most part, Japanese Americans found acceptance in Cincinnati's neighborhoods and in the workplace.

By the early winter months of 1943, some U.S. soldiers had already been forced to endure a second holiday season away from their families. Attitudes about the war slowly changed. Americans remained optimistic that the Allies would be victorious, but they were less sure about how long the process would take. A new expression—"for the duration"—now entered into the home front lexicon. A curious and often contradictory set of emotions was on display. Americans grumbled about shortages, blackouts and all the disruptions the war had ushered in. At the same time, the American people knew that their sacrifices were linked to the larger war effort. In the fall of 1943, both UC and XU suspended most varsity-level athletics. Annual summer festivals were put on hold. One parish, St. James in White Oak, suspended formal plans for its centennial anniversary. Church leaders expressed a fervent wish that the war would end soon: "Let us hope history repeats itself. The Diamond Jubilee of St. James was celebrated in 1918 during World War I. In November it came to an end. Now in 1943 we are celebrating the centennial jubilee. Here's hoping World War II will end this year."

The shortage of fuel, food and people to perform the necessary tasks of a wartime economy led to even more changes in the day-to-day lives of Cincinnatians in 1943. In the city where professional baseball got its start, Cincinnatians had long associated the thaw of winter in February and

March with spring training. Since 1931, members of the Cincinnati Reds had reported to a spring training facility in Tampa, Florida, to prepare for the upcoming season. Due to chronic fuel shortages, the Office of Defense Transportation determined that baseball teams could no longer travel to distant locations for spring training. The Reds and several other major league clubs found suitable practice facilities in Indiana. Starting in 1943 and continuing for the war's duration, the Reds began their seasons in the sleepy college town of Bloomington, Indiana, home to the University of Indiana (IU) campus. The players lodged at the nearby Graham Hotel and walked over to train on IU's Jordan Field. Rain proved to be the team's greatest adversary during spring training. Nine of its first ten practices had to be held indoors. Determined to manage a winning team, Deacon Bill McKechnie contracted the services of Bill Miller, also known as the "muscle magician," to whip his players into shape. Miller ran the players through an innovative regimen of stretching and rhythmic motions to limber up their muscles. That year, in Bloomington, the Reds' trainer, Matty Schaub, discovered a talented student athlete named Ted Kluszewski who had been hired to help prepare the training facilities for the Reds. While Kluszewski's proven talents were on the gridiron as a tight end for the IU squad, Schaub was duly impressed when he witnessed Kluszewski's knack for hitting balls over the fences of the practice field. Kluszewski, of course, was eventually signed by the Reds and became a mainstay with the club in the 1950s.

When the baseball season began in 1943, the Reds adjusted start times for many home games so that second- and third-shift workers could attend an occasional game. Despite these efforts, attendance for the season suffered. In a similar fashion, the Archdiocese of Cincinnati allowed many of its parishes to adopt the practice of offering midnight Masses on Saturday night so its Catholic parishioners would have more options to juggle church attendance around their busy workweeks.

By the spring and summer of 1943, it had become clear to many Queen City residents that food shortages were here to stay. More than 25 percent of commercially grown produce was sent to military bases or shipped overseas to feed the troops. To offset these shortages, the federal government promoted the idea of planting victory gardens. The precedent for victory gardens dates back to the Great War. The Wilson administration had proposed a similar initiative during World War I. During that conflict, the federal government supplied information, guidance and encouragement to city residents who were not familiar with the "how tos" of planting and cultivating a garden. A variation of that wartime program sprang up during the lean years of

By the spring of 1943, the Office of Defense Transportation had placed strict limits on where professional baseball teams could practice during their exhibition seasons. As a result, the Reds trained in nearby Bloomington, Indiana, for three years. *Courtesy of Public Library of Cincinnati and Hamilton County.*

the Great Depression. In Cincinnati, for example, officials encouraged city dwellers to tend community gardens on unused plots of city land. Many of these community gardens became victory gardens during the war. The Department of Agriculture funneled its sage advice for successful gardening through the HCNDC. In order to whip up support for victory gardens, such

Locally, an estimated seventy thousand gardens existed in Hamilton County by 1943. In many cases, area companies allowed employees to tend communal gardens located on their property during nonworking hours. *Courtesy of Public Library of Cincinnati and Hamilton County.*

slogans as "food fights for freedom" and "vegetables for victory" became commonly heard. The *Cincinnati Post* did not mince words in a January 1943 article: "It's only fair to warn you that you are going to grow very weary of the limited diet that will be yours unless you make plans, now, for some way of supplementing what will be available in the stores."

In addition to the obvious benefits that a victory garden might yield, government officials promoted the program as a way to "maintain and improve the morale and spiritual well-being of the individual, family, and Nation."

Following Allied successes in North Africa in 1942, British and American forces engaged in a joint offensive in Sicily and Italy, what Churchill referred to as "the soft underbelly of Europe." Ultimately, the British and Americans were preparing a larger plan to train troops for a cross-channel invasion of Nazi-occupied France. Such an invasion would help take the pressure off Soviet troops, who had been bearing a disproportionate share of the fighting against Nazi Germany since Hitler invaded Russia in June 1941. Beginning in 1942, American convoys transported men and equipment to Great Britain. Throughout 1943, the Big Three Allied leaders, Roosevelt, Churchill and Stalin, discussed the ideal circumstances and timing for such a cross-channel invasion. Roosevelt named General Dwight David Eisenhower, one of the rising stars of the U.S. high command, as supreme Allied commander of the operation. Incoming U.S. forces transformed portions of Great Britain into a vast military base to train for the upcoming offensive. Meanwhile, U.S. forces in the Pacific continued to meet with success against Imperial Japan.

From the onset of America's involvement in the war, the Roosevelt administration made it clear that the success of the nation was inextricably tied to the successes enjoyed by the Allies. Lend-lease aid continued to flow toward Great Britain, the Soviet Union and China to assist each nation in its efforts to defeat the Axis powers. In addition to promoting and maintaining home front morale, the OWI also had the responsibility of casting America's allies in the best possible light. In scores of films approved by the OWI, American audiences were reminded about the virtues of its allies and the vile aspects of its enemies. Feature films like *Mrs. Miniver* and *The North Star* reinforced the democratic values of the British and even the Russians. In its depiction of the enemy, the OWI approved a few rare films—*Casablanca* and *The Moon Is Down*—that allowed for the distinction between the "good German" and the evil Nazi. Films set in the Pacific were less forgiving and, frankly, more racist in their depiction of the enemy. Combat movies such as *So Proudly We Hail* and *The Purple Heart* highlighted the worst stereotypes of the Japanese people: a cunning, diabolical, sadistic, ruthless enemy, utterly devoid of any redeeming characteristics whatsoever.

The government-endorsed efforts about U.S. allies did not go unnoticed in Cincinnati. Eugene Goosens, conductor of the Cincinnati Symphony Orchestra, kicked off the 1942–43 season in October with a series of weekly concerts that paid tribute to the various members of the united nations. Each concert performance opened with the playing of the national anthem and included a "fanfare" dedicated to one of America's allies. The first three concerts, predictably, paid tribute to America's major allies. On subsequent weeks, Goosens dedicated fanfares to other countries that had pledged their support against the Axis powers. He also devoted musical tributes to each branch of the armed forces, including less recognized groups such as the Coast Guard and the Merchant Marines. One notable omission concerned women. Although WACS and WAVES had entered the women's auxiliary branches

Eugene Goosens came to Cincinnati from the Rochester Philharmonic Orchestra. He conducted the CSO from 1931 until 1946. In addition to "Fanfare for the Common Man," Goosens also had the good fortune to present the world premiere of an additional work by Aaron Copeland, *Lincoln Portrait*, in March 1942. *Courtesy of the University of Adelaide Library (Series 312).*

of the army and navy in sizeable numbers by 1943, no musical tributes were dedicated to these deserving individuals. Near the end of the 1942–43 season, on March 12, 1943, Goosens and the CSO performed a world premiere of Aaron Copeland's *Fanfare for the Common Man*. Goosens had asked the renowned composer to write a composition to complement the fanfares paying tribute to the united nations and the troops. Copeland's composition may be the closest thing to a wartime anthem that acknowledged the sacrifices that had already been given and for ones yet to be made during this epic struggle.

Another Cincinnatian moved to action was Reverend Nelson Burroughs, rector at Christ Church. In October 1942, he expressed the desire for his church to convert its chapel into a tribute to America's allies. In February 1943, Christ Church dedicated its United Nations Chapel. Church members generously donated funds so that flags representing each of America's allies could be displayed. Members donated funds to sponsor thirty flags, each uniform in size, three by five feet, representing the various countries that had taken the pledge to defeat the Axis powers. Burroughs hoped that the newly dedicated chapel could also serve as a public place for prayer for the entire city. The prayer corner, in the westernmost corner of the chapel, proudly displayed an honor roll of the 224 church members who were currently in the military. Bishop Hobson donated the use of a wood carving of the Christ figure, sculpted by Swiss artist Anton Fritz. While the carving may have been mistaken for a crucifix, Burroughs explained that "in Christ Church we emphasize the living Christ, triumphant, compassionate!" Burroughs made arrangements for Michael Coleman, an Episcopalian minister from London, to speak at the dedication event. Coleman's church had been destroyed by German bombs during the Blitz. Burroughs also invited representatives of the Allied nations to attend and encouraged any Cincinnati resident with a relative in the service to come as well. Thousands of Cincinnatians made their way to Christ Church's prayer corner before the war ended.

On occasion, city leaders had the opportunity to pay tribute to America's allies. In May 1943, Mayor Stewart used the ceremonial powers of his office to proclaim "Russia Day." In a similar fashion, in January 1944, UC president Raymond Walters put the spotlight of the university on Great Britain. Walters invited Viscount Halifax, Great Britain's ambassador to the United States, to attend the university's midyear commencement ceremonies. Walters bestowed an honorary degree on the visiting dignitary.

Not all Cincinnatians, of course, expressed positive views of the Allied powers. In May 1943, Hollywood released the feature film *Mission to Moscow*.

Miss Lenora C. Faulwetter,
628 W. 5th St.,
Covington, Ky.

CHRIST CHURCH BULLETIN

CINCINNATI

SEPTUAGESIMA SUNDAY

Vol. 2   FEBRUARY 21, 1943   No. 8

**The Reverend
Michael
Coleman**

**Vicar of
All Hallows' By
the Tower
of
London**

No one who was present last year, when Dr. Coleman preached in Christ Church, will ever forget the sermon he gave us. He is, first of all, a man of profound faith, devout and good. He has seen his historic church destroyed, for it fell during the German blitz of December, 1940. He went through that hell, night after night, with his people. He was their padré, ministering to them in life and death. His is "faith under fire."

We are the most fortunate parish in the world, to be able to have this modern Christian saint, fresh from the field of battle, as our guest on the occasion when we dedicate our Prayer Corner, and the flags of the United Nations. Invite your friends—5 o'clock Sunday afternoon.

Thirty groups and individuals donated funds to purchase flags for the United Nations Chapel. These flags remained on display at Christ Church Cathedral until 2004. *Courtesy of Christ Church Cathedral Archives.*

Opposite: Christ Church invited Reverend Michael Coleman, the vicar of All Hallows Church in London, to address the church when it dedicated the United Nations Chapel. *Courtesy of Christ Church Cathedral Archives.*

The film had the support of President Roosevelt because the script depicted the Soviet allies in an extremely positive light. One Cincinnati resident, Robert Steiger, of 666 State Street, objected to the film's premise. He wrote

Christ Church hired Paul Briol, a prominent local photographer, to create this alluring photo composition for the dedication of the United Nations Chapel and prayer corner. Parishioner Edith Howard kneels at the prayer rail. Briol superimposed images of Howard's two sons—William, who was serving in the army, and Lee, who had enlisted in the navy. Both sons survived the conflict. *Courtesy of Christ Church Cathedral Archives.*

a scathing letter to the editor of the *Times-Star*: "The aid which Russia has given the Allied cause by her heroic resistance to the Nazis in eastern Europe is recognized by all of us, but we Americans are just about fed up with those elements which are trying to force Russian communism upon us in the guise

At the university's 1944 winter commencement exercises, University of Cincinnati president Raymond Walters (right) conferred an honorary LLD on Viscount Halifax, Great Britain's ambassador to the United States. *Courtesy of University of Cincinnati Archives.*

of true democracy. They [the Soviets] are just as much a menace to us as the Nazi agents who are operating in the United States."

Steiger hoped his comments might close down the film's run in the Queen City. He added: "Cincinnatians should see to it that this piece of subversive propaganda does not appear in our local motion picture houses, and all loyal Americans should try to have it scrapped."

At least one other Queen City resident agreed with Steiger. In remarks prepared for the General Federation of Women's Clubs, Raymond Walters noted that the Soviet Union was ideologically closer to the Axis powers than the united nations: "It may be granted that democracy is slow and inefficient. But we need not feel sad about comparing its total result with the dictatorial swiftness and the brutal competency of the modern collectivist, whether of Hitler's Germany or of Mussolini's Italy or of Soviet Russia under Stalin."

In May 1943, the long-standing antiwar group Mothers of Sons, organized to oppose the federal government's efforts to institute the draft, conducted a two-hour meeting at the Hotel Gibson. Mrs. Lucinda Benge, the group's leader, faulted nearly every aspect of President Roosevelt's conduct as commander in chief. She was convinced that the president's "total war" rhetoric was nothing more than a naked power grab that would only oppress the American people. Benge pointedly observed:

> *In all of the administration plans of government control of education, labor and capital, the Hitlerian motif stands out—domination of the state over every phase of national life…We are hearing constantly the pleas for "All-out War,"—all-out of the country for boys, all-out of business for small business, all-out of rest and freedom for the rank and file and all-out of money due to high taxes for working people.*

Mothers of Sons continued to meet occasionally throughout the year. The leaders used these meetings to encourage their members to write letters to their government representatives. Clearly, this group was out of sync with the views of most of its contemporaries. Unlike the majority of Americans, or Cincinnatians for that matter, Mothers of Sons never strayed from its strict adherence to isolationism. Moreover, the group remained distrustful of the faith that Roosevelt placed in the Grand Alliance. Regrettably, its anti-British and anti-Soviet rhetoric was usually coupled with its anti-Semitic views. In her May 11 speech, Benge noted: "We have no stake in North Africa or Europe…The people are sick and tired at this doting attitude toward Britain at our expense. We call for an end to this subservience to Britain…Let the Jews fight their own war in Europe—Our war is in the Pacific."

To be sure, the Grand Alliance had its faults. The Soviet Union was not a natural ally of the United States. Churchill and Roosevelt did not always see eye to eye on strategy and tactics. But the Allies overcame their differences and began to meet with success. Following the successful Russian defense of Stalingrad, the Soviet Red Army launched a determined counteroffensive against Nazi forces. American and British forces combined to defeat the joint German and Italian troops on the Italian Peninsula.

Halfway around the world, the U.S. victory at Guadalcanal in February 1943 continued to shrink the area in the Pacific controlled by Imperial Japan. These critical military developments led to important changes on the American home front. On November 1, 1943, the War Department officially recommended that all state and local defense councils suspend air raid drills indefinitely. While Pentagon officials conceded that "token air raids are always a possibility...the present degree of danger" was regarded as minimal.

Many of the sixty thousand residents who had volunteered and trained for the enemy invasions of the home front that never transpired began to repurpose their efforts. One outlet for the energies of home front volunteers lay in the need for quality childcare. One of the most thorough revolutionary changes ushered in during the war years had to do with the dramatic surge of women in the paid workforce. With men enlisting or responding to their draft notices in record numbers, large vacancies existed in industries vital to the war effort. The OWI worked with the War Manpower Commission (WMC) to coordinate publicity campaigns such as the iconic poster of "Rosie the Riveter," with the tag line "We can do it," to encourage traditional housewives—married women and women with children—to work outside the home. The campaign worked. In 1943 alone, Crosley Radio replaced more than eight hundred positions that had been previously held by men with women. According to a January 1943 WMC report, more than twenty-eight thousand women in Greater Cincinnati worked in the paid labor force. Before the end of the year, the number of Cincinnati "Rosies" had increased to nearly fifty thousand. In December 1943, the HCNDC began a partnership with Elizabeth Dyer, dean of UC's College of Home Economics, to chair an Emergency Committee on Child Care. Dyer helped coordinate the efforts of twenty-seven day nurseries in Hamilton County. Many of these nurseries had operated for years during the Depression under the auspices of the Works Progress Administration. These nurseries met the needs of nearly 1,100 children. While these figures may sound paltry, they reflect the fact that most American women in the 1940s preferred to rely on friends, neighbors and extended family to care for their children instead of group care facilities.

With the exception of air raid drills, which effectively ended in late 1943, Cincinnati's home front dutifully supported the war effort for the duration

Elizabeth Dyer served as dean of the College of Home Economics at the University of Cincinnati for nearly four decades. During the war years, she helped working women find the support services they needed to hold down jobs and tend to their families. *Courtesy of University of Cincinnati Archives.*

of the fighting. As more of Cincinnati's sons and daughters entered into the armed services, their friends and family members at home had even more motivation and incentive to do everything in their power to help push the war to a speedy and successful end. In January 1944, Harold Nichols, now Ohio's state salvage chairman, promoted a one-day waste-paper scrap drive in this way: "On the battle fronts, the drive goes forward incessantly and here on the home front, we can't slacken our efforts, either…We have to have scrap paper to keep the stream of supplies flowing to the boys on the battle front."

Cincinnatians continued to do their bit—buying war bonds, participating in salvage drives, growing victory gardens and performing necessary war work—all in the belief that their efforts were contributing to the defeat of the Axis powers.

Chapter 4

THOSE WHO SERVED

CINCINNATIANS IN UNIFORM 1941–44

World War II surpassed the Great War and every other military conflict in terms of the war's demands on the civilian population. Since the onset of fighting in Europe and Asia in the 1930s, the distinction between military and civilian targets had been blurred beyond recognition. By 1942, the Axis powers had overrun and successfully occupied most of Europe, North Africa, portions of the Middle East and Asia. The united nations that banded against those aggressor nations were expected to mobilize their full industrial and productive potentials for war. Total war demanded total commitment and total sacrifice. By 1943, the leaders of the Grand Alliance had come to agree that by adhering to the demands of total war, nothing less than unconditional surrender of the Axis powers would be tolerated.

While the leaders of the Grand Alliance may have spoken about the shared and collective burdens of total war, Churchill and Stalin understood war in absolute terms. The Blitz of London in 1940 and the heroic defense of Stalingrad in 1942–43 were tangible and real reminders of total sacrifice. The United States, on the other hand, engaged in this war differently. In fact, the American experience during World War II rested on the basic premise that wars were fought on foreign soil. World War II conformed to that logic. The government mobilized its citizenry, trained those recruits at military bases and then shipped them abroad to combat zones in foreign lands. Since the United States engaged repeatedly in foreign wars, it could recover from these conflicts faster than if they had been fought on American soil. President Roosevelt talked extensively about total war, but the actual level of America's sacrifice, in terms of material costs and human lives, paled in comparison to most of the other belligerent nations. Russian, German, French and British soldiers were defending their homes, unlike their American counterparts. Nonetheless, this generation that served their country believed that America's role in this war was both necessary and just.

For the second time in the twentieth century, the United States government passed legislation that created a military draft. The Selective Service Act of 1940, the first peacetime draft in our nation's history, initially targeted native-born and immigrant men between the ages of eighteen and thirty-six years. Draftees would be trained and expected to serve for a period of one year. When the United States became a belligerent power, the draft range was broadened to include men up to forty-five years of age. Terms of service were lengthened indefinitely—that is, for the duration of the conflict.

Eventually, women were permitted to volunteer for military service. Army chief of staff General George C. Marshall threw his support behind the idea of women joining the ranks of the armed forces, although strictly as noncombatants. The Women's Army Corps (WACS) provided women with the first chance to enlist in 1942. Each of the other branches soon followed suit. Women ended up doing everything short of fighting; they served as nurses, file clerks and even test pilots. Eventually, opportunities for service in auxiliary branches of the army, navy, Marine Corps and the Coast Guard opened up to them. Whatever their level of contribution, the idea was simple. Each woman in uniform allowed another man to be available for combat duty. By the end of the war, some fifteen million American men and women served their nation in the armed forces. This cumulative total represented 11.4 percent of the overall population compared to 4.6 percent during the previous conflict.

Cincinnati provided its fair share of citizen soldiers for military service. In 1940, during the first round of the draft, more than eighty-one thousand Hamilton County residents registered with local draft boards. Some men who worked in vital industries received deferments. A few courageous Cincinnatians who adhered to pacifist ideals asked their local draft boards to classify them as conscientious objectors. The federal government was determined not to repeat the mistakes of World War I when citizens with genuine moral objections to war had been forced to serve, sometimes as combatants. In May 1941, the *Cincinnati Post* reported that six draftees in Hamilton County had asked to be classified as conscientious objectors. In each case, the draftee's church interceded on his behalf. The churches negotiated a plan of alternative service with local draft officials. The churches agreed to cover the costs of sending their charges to a special camp where they would work on reforestation and soil conservation projects. Lieutenant Colonel Chester Goble, the state director of selective service, weighed in on the matter: "They [the churches] feel that while their church members cannot conscientiously accept military training, they are doing a patriotic service in working for the national welfare."

During the period of defense mobilization, the federal government sought out and recruited the talents of individuals with specialized medical training. In the summer of 1941, area physicians at Cincinnati's General Hospital responded generously to a call from the surgeon general of the U.S. Army to set up a General Hospital Unit. A similar unit, the Twenty-fifth General Hospital Unit, had served the men of the American Expeditionary Forces in France during World War I. The U.S. Army recommissioned the unit. The Twenty-fifth eventually saw extensive action in France and Belgium following the successful invasion of France in 1944. Other Cincinnati doctors shared their expertise with the armed forces in a variety of ways. Dr. Frank Mayfield headed the neurosurgery program at Percy Jones Hospital in Battle Creek, Michigan, where he conducted research on soldiers with nerve injuries. Dr. Albert Sabin served as a lieutenant colonel in the U.S. Army Medical Corps. He provided strategies for dealing with infectious diseases in both the Sicilian Campaign in 1943 and, later on, in the Pacific theater. The army awarded Sabin the Legion of Merit for his important contributions. In fact, 6 percent of the nation's doctors decorated for meritorious service were affiliated with UC's College of Medicine.

During the early days of war, eager men crowded into recruiting offices. Each branch of the armed forces experienced a mad rush of young men ready to enlist. Potter Stewart, son of Cincinnati mayor James G. Stewart, and one of the charter members of Yale University's America First Committee, went to the nearest naval recruiting office to enlist. Before long, all three of Senator Robert Taft's sons enlisted in various branches of the armed forces. John Gilligan, son of Harry Gilligan, the volunteer commander of Cincinnati's air raid wardens, interrupted his religious studies at Notre Dame University to enlist in the navy. Countless other Cincinnatians responded to the U.S. entry into the war in this manner.

On December 11, 1941, the day Germany declared war on the United States and just four days after the attack on Pearl Harbor, UC president Raymond Walters addressed the men's convocation at Wilson Auditorium. He empathized with the young men of draft age who were eager to support the war. At the same time, he urged students to avoid making impulsive or emotional decisions when it came to their academic careers. "The important thing," he advised, "is that you should act, not upon the spur of emotionalism, or war hysteria, but upon careful thought as to where you will be of most use to the country." Officials at Xavier University offered similar advice to their student body. In a pamphlet entitled *Xavier University in a World at War* (1942), university officials compiled quotes from leading civilian and military officials in the federal government. The pamphlet encouraged male students to maintain their studies. Colonel C.W. Venable, speaking on behalf of the U.S. Army in January 1942, had this to say:

> *The basic qualities of a good soldier are no different from those of a good citizen. We need men of good professional training, and good physical development, and character. The soldier should have a clear-cut idea of what is right and what is wrong. He must have training, foresight, and ability to form a conviction for which he will die. He needs instruction in the obligations of citizenship.*

Area universities did their best to accommodate the changing needs of their male students. During the remainder of the 1941–42 academic year, officials endeavored to accelerate curriculums for upper classmen in order to increase the likelihood of their graduation before they were drafted. As the manpower needs of the armed forces increased, the roles that Cincinnati's universities played in supporting the war effort would also change dramatically.

Eventually, every neighborhood, church community, school and place of employment in Cincinnati was directly affected by the void left by men either replying to their draft notice or enlisting. The War and Navy Departments determined that families who had family members actively serving in the armed forces were entitled to display a service star banner in the front window of their houses. The idea of the service star banner originated in Ohio during World War I, patented by a father who had two sons serving in the Ohio Fifth Infantry. During World War II, the War and Navy Departments restored that tradition. In addition to the service star banners, family members of servicemen and women were also allowed to wear service star lapel pins. Typically, the banners consisted of a blue star on a white field. Although companies produced banners commercially, many were homemade creations. Their appearance varied from one community to the next. When servicemen were listed as wartime casualties, their families displayed a gold star in place of the regular service star. The gold star served as a somber reminder of the sacrifices implicit in the war. It also alerted neighbors about the family's and community's loss. When the duration of the war stretched over several years, "Gold Star Mothers" sadly became more common in Cincinnati neighborhoods.

These talismans—banners and lapel pins—fit within a larger cultural context of a nation engaged in all-out war. Women who volunteered as nurses' aides or as USO workers often donned uniforms. Harry Gilligan assumed the rank of "commander" among his volunteer corps of air raid wardens. War workers proudly wore "E" pins when their companies received recognition for their excellent work. Homeowners hung "V Home" banners in the front windows, proving that they had complied with air raid precautions and other war-related measures. Uniformed military attachés from various branches of the armed forces made timely appearances at war bond rallies and salvage drives to remind civilians that their commonplace efforts had a direct bearing on the war at the front lines. Service stars represented yet one more way in which the federal government could convey its vision of shared sacrifice with the American people.

By promoting morale and encouraging supportive actions, the Roosevelt administration, through federal agencies like the Office of War Information (OWI) and the Office of Civilian Defense (OCD), hoped to maintain high levels of public engagement. The former agency generated the content, or information, while the latter distributed it through its vast network of state and local defense councils. The White House's careful management of war information meant that the administration, its war aims and its allies were usually portrayed in a positive light. World War II, however, was a "censored war" for other reasons.

Wartime propaganda, in the form of posters, radio scripts and motion pictures, emphasized the connections between everyday actions and their consequences. The truly effective practitioners of this messaging found ways to show how the average citizen's thoughts and actions impacted the troops' well-being. One OWI-approved poster that promoted the idea of carpooling depicted the face of a war-weary, unshaven GI. It offered the following scold: "Have you really tried to save gas by joining a car club?" Many posters warned against spreading rumors or engaging in defeatist talk. These posters contained some variation of a simple and powerful message: "Loose lips sink ships," "loose tweets sink fleets" or "loose talk can cost lives." One of the most poignant OWI posters showed a gold star banner in the background and a lonely puppy waiting for the master who would never return. Draped under the dog was the collar of the dead sailor's uniform. The terse message at the bottom of the poster read, "Because someone talked."

Even though the home front was inundated with news from the fighting fronts, most Americans at home viewed the war through a sterile and sanitized lens. To be sure, journalists and photographers documented World War II unlike any other war. War correspondents embedded in combat units provided a steady diet of stories from the front lines, along with still photos of the war for newspapers and magazines and moving images for newsreels. For the first two and a half years of the war, however, the Roosevelt administration kept a tight lid on images of dead American soldiers. In the fall of 1943, the OWI finally authorized the first release of still images of dead American GIs. The September 20, 1943 issue of *Life* magazine ran a photo of three dead Americans who died during an amphibious landing on a beach at Papua, New Guinea. The limp bodies lay face down in the sand, their identities obscured. The actual invasion had transpired the previous February. President Roosevelt authorized the release of this photo at that moment only because he feared that the home front was growing complacent about the growing demands of total war.

Throughout the war, even when support for some of the home front initiatives and programs waned, public concern for the men and women in uniform seldom wavered. Through a variety of methods, Cincinnatians maintained close connections with friends, relatives and neighbors who went off to serve their country. Employers kept tabs on former employees by publishing company newsletters. Schools and churches posted bulletins with articles about their members who had answered the call. In a similar vein, concerned citizens found ways to keep servicemen up to date with neighborhood and community news. In the spring and summer of 1942, Dorothy Snowden Rowe, mother of an enlistee, developed a newsletter for the servicemen of Indian Hill Chapel, the church she and her family attended. She wanted to pass along all the hometown news to her son and his friends and neighbors. In this way, she hoped the newsletter might help ward off any homesickness they might experience. Some of Rowe's neighbors helped defray the costs of this local publication, named the *Carrier Pigeon*. In October 1942, the first edition of the *Carrier Pigeon* went out to 141 servicemen from Rowe's church community. Soon the newsletter reached soldiers in military camps all over the United States and in the theaters of combat. Many of the recipients of the newsletter wrote back to Mrs. Rowe. Under the watchful dictates of military censors, servicemen could write only about their experiences in generic terms. They were forbidden to reveal specific locations of their units in any correspondence sent home. This newsletter and others like it helped maintain the morale of those on the

As more and more men went off to war, the attention of the home front remained focused on those individuals. *Courtesy of University of Cincinnati Archives.*

home front as well as those on the front line. In a slim, self-published 1963 memoir, Rowe said her work on the *Carrier Pigeon* "was probably the most satisfactory thing I ever wrote." She added that it "was the most rewarding war work I could have chosen."

Many Cincinnatians sent letters and packages to keep in touch with servicemen and women. The steady decrease in male students at area universities provided options for some female students to step in and help out. Because Xavier University and UC closed most of their fraternities for the duration, women occasionally helped operate those groups while the men were away. At Xavier University, for example, several women served in temporary leadership roles at the Kappa Sigma Mu fraternity. These women took it upon themselves to send care packages to former Xavier students who had become GIs. These packages also contained letters of the current news at Xavier. Letters coming back from grateful servicemen exuded a sense of optimism about the Allied war effort, with some signing their letters "Yours in Victory." Letters written to people in the service certainly boosted their spirits. The return letters from servicemen and women provided Cincinnatians with new perspectives about the sorts of demands that were being placed on members of the armed forces.

On December 10, 1942, one soldier wrote back from a Pennsylvania training camp, expressing his appreciation for receiving a package of "Christmas cheer." He noted that "it certainly makes you feel good to get mail from a source that was always near and dear to your heart...Get the members [of the fraternity] to write to us in [the] service as it really lightens the load we are all carrying."

Two Xavier soldiers wrote home from military bases in California. One serviceman stationed at an army air corps base near San Francisco complained about the "disagreeable climate" and mosquitoes. Private Harry Weber, who was training to become a weather observer for the army, reported his good fortune of going to the Hollywood Canteen, one of the more famous places in Southern California that extended hospitality to visiting GIs. He met several stars of the screen such as actor Fred MacMurry, actress Heddy LaMarr, actor and singer Rudy Valley and big bandleader Kay Kyser.

Yet another soldier who wrote home to his friends seemed to be more mindful of changes the war had wrought. He expressed contradictory emotions, welcoming new opportunities while feeling slightly overwhelmed with the new responsibilities that had been thrust on him. As a newly commissioned second lieutenant, he noted, "The pressure becomes heavier.

THE CARRIER PIGEON
from The Indian Hill Chapel

| JAN, 10, 1943 | INDIAN HILL, OHIO | NO. 3 |

Charles Dana Gibson, a famous illustrator and the creator of the popular "Gibson Girl" images, agreed to make the masthead for Dorothy Rowe's newsletter called the *Carrier Pigeon*. From the summer of 1942 until the end of the war, Rowe sent out monthly newsletters with the help of her Indian Hill church members who were serving in the armed forces. *Courtesy of Indian Hill Historical Society*.

Being responsible for the lives of about fifty men is no small job." He concluded his letter with the following appeal:

> *I'm asking a special favor of all of you who are keeping our homes warm, safe, and happy and that is to remember me often in your prayers, not so much for myself but that I have the strength, the wisdom, and grace, to bring back from the battlefield the boys who will be looking to me and trusting me to bring them back to a kind of life they left at home.*

Laura May Weber, an American Red Cross volunteer, corresponded with her friends at Kappa Sigma Mu. After receiving orientation training as a Red Cross Recreation Worker in February 1942, she was assigned to duty aboard a naval hospital ship in Norfolk, Virginia. She stated with some pride that "Norfolk is a real Navy town with everyone in uniform—even we, in the Red Cross, must wear uniforms on the compound." Her duties as a Red Cross volunteer included making arrangements for performers to come to the hospital for shows, orchestrating handicrafts for the patients and organizing dances for those who were physically able to participate.

Letter writing also played an important role in the efforts of one church community to reach out and care for Italian prisoners of war. In the fall of 1942, more than seven hundred Italian sailors had been captured by Allied forces at the conclusion of the North African campaign. The prisoners had been transported to the United States and held at a military facility in Salina, Texas. Father Richard Secchia, the pastor of Cincinnati's Sacred Heart parish, spearheaded a letter-writing campaign among his parishioners. Sacred Heart's congregation was made up mostly of first- and second-generation Italian Americans who still had strong familial ties to their homeland. In addition to their letters, beginning in 1943, church members also assembled and sent men's toiletries and other comfort items as a form of ministry for the POWs.

<hr />

Altogether, Cincinnati's college campuses experienced profound changes during the war. All three Cincinnati universities felt the impact of the war on their daily operations. Enrollments at each of the universities fluctuated wildly as men went off to war. The rabbinical school at Hebrew Union College, the city's smallest and most specialized institution of higher learning, had the unique distinction of providing the highest per capita number of chaplains in the country to the various branches of the armed forces. On the other hand, Xavier's ability to keep its doors open seemed genuinely in doubt by 1943. The previous year had witnessed a temporary surge in student population. The vast majority of the resident students in Evanston had joined the enlisted reserve corps. By January 1943, however, those students were called to active duty. According to XU president Father Celestin J. Steiner, the university had but two options: close its doors for the duration or secure a contract to train troops. At this time, officials in the federal Selective Service Administration were lobbying for programs that would help young draftees and enlistees complete their college education since each branch of the armed forces needed well-educated men to fill out the officers' ranks.

In February 1943, the army air corps announced that Xavier would serve as an officer training center. It was among 281 universities to perform such a function. Approximately 260 air cadets arrived from Maxwell Air Force Base by bus in March as part of the army air corps' College Training Detachment (CTD) program. A second cohort of 250 cadets arrived one month later. Likewise, of the 486 universities chosen by the U.S. Army to educate its personnel, two of the locations for the Army Service Training Program (ASTP) happened to be local: both Xavier and the University of Cincinnati would serve as hosts for this program.

The arrival of the soldiers transformed both campuses. During the academic year 1943–44, nearly 2,500 ASTP soldiers took classes at UC. University officials emptied out classrooms, faculty offices and eight fraternity houses near the campus to house the new arrivals. McMicken Hall, one of the oldest buildings on the UC campus, was converted into a military barracks. Life for these student-soldiers was highly structured. From dawn to dusk, they busied themselves with early morning exercises and a full day of classwork, often followed by guard duty. CTD and ASTP regulations prevented the cadets from participating in collegiate athletics. One air cadet who transferred to Xavier to complete his CTD training recalled that the emphasis was entirely on secular education. "The Jesuit brothers," he noted, "were conscientious about teaching the courses and did not emphasize religion or try to convert any of the non-Catholic cadets." Cadets who were training to become pilots, navigators and bombardiers took classes in math,

This page and next: In 1943 and 1944, two programs from the army and the army air corps sent soldiers to Xavier University to complete work on their college studies. These cadets swelled the ranks of the student body and transformed the campus in countless ways. *Courtesy of Xavier University Archives.*

Army cadets march in file at Xavier University. Sometimes the cadets drilled on the streets around Xavier's campus near nightfall. City manager Sherrill encouraged the trainees to march with lanterns in order to prevent traffic accidents. *Courtesy of Xavier University Archives.*

physics, history and geometry. A friendly rivalry existed on the XU campus between the two groups of future soldiers and airmen. The air cadets proved to be exceptional in one important way. Two dogs wandered onto the XU campus after the arrival of the CTD cadets. The men adopted the dogs as their mascots. Jughead, a medium-sized mixed breed, and GI, a "mostly" German shepherd, ate in the dining hall with the cadets, slept with them in their dorm rooms and even attended classes with the men.

Officials in Washington, D.C., had been under pressure to curtail the CTD and ASTP programs. By 1944, the need for trained pilots had lessened. Officials argued that too many young men had been channeled into college classrooms for training. This meant that older men, especially men with dependents, had been filling the void. The army and the army air corps suspended these training programs abruptly in the spring of 1944. Both Xavier and UC had benefitted from the military training programs. Raymond Walters expressed doubts about the future for both Xavier and the University of Cincinnati. Without federal assistance, he declared, it was hard to imagine how either institution could remain solvent. Congress, however, was already at work on a plan to assist returning servicemen and women to the classroom.

As local men and women continued to answer the call to serve in the armed forces, those individuals who remained at home paid closer attention to war news from the fighting fronts. Cincinnatians received steady doses of information each day in the morning and evening newspapers. Radio broadcasts complemented print media. With each trip to the neighborhood theater, Cincinnatians viewed newsreels that provided a summary overview of the week's events. Concerned parents, siblings, neighbors and sweethearts watched and listened for any news about their loved ones.

On occasion, stories of soldiers who had ties to Cincinnati captured the attention of the national media. Such was the case when news of the tragic death of Alexander Goode was made public. Goode, who was born in Brooklyn, New York, and raised in Washington, D.C., had two connections to the Queen City. After earning an undergraduate degree from the University of Cincinnati, he studied to become a rabbi at Hebrew Union College. Goode applied to become a naval chaplain in 1942, shortly after Pearl Harbor was attacked. In February 1943, Goode and three other chaplains—two Protestant ministers and one Catholic priest—were assigned to the U.S. Army Transport (USAT) *Dorchester*, a troop transport ship. On January 23, 1943, the *Dorchester* joined a convoy departing from New York on its way to Greenland. Commanders of the mission knew the risks that faced them. German U-boats menaced the waters of the North Atlantic on a regular basis. On the night of February 3, the *Dorchester* suffered catastrophic injuries when it was torpedoed by a German submarine. Goode and the other chaplains gave their life vests to frightened seamen and helped the crew into lifeboats. Survivors of the ordeal recalled hearing a mixture of spoken Hebrew Jewish and Latin Catholic prayers as the four chaplains faced their deaths aboard the sinking craft.

As wartime casualties mounted, many Cincinnati churches began the practice of offering up prayers and petitions for those in uniform at their weekly services. Some churches took an additional step, dedicating war memorials to

On July 11, 1943, Xavier officials dedicated a memorial to its students and faculty who were serving in the armed forces. Archbishop McNicholas blessed the Shrine of Our Lady, Queen of Victory and Peace. *Courtesy of Xavier University Archives.*

honor the service of active military personnel as well as those who had paid the ultimate sacrifice. On July 11, 1943, the religious community at Xavier University dedicated the Shrine of Our Lady, Queen of Victory and Peace. Each day in October 1943, a contingent of the XU student body, including air cadets, walked down to the shrine and prayed the rosary. The group expressed the hope that through its actions it could maintain "a union of prayer with X-men in the service throughout the world." During the spring of 1944, the parish at St. John the Evangelist, in Deer Park, converted its Lourdes grotto into a "service shrine" to honor the 265 men and women in the service from its congregation. At the time of the shrine's installation, three of the parish's churchgoers had died in the war.

There was one final way in which Cincinnatians maintained a bond with those in the service. A few months after the draft went into operation, Franklin Roosevelt encouraged various groups to pool their collective resources to help create much-needed recreational facilities for troops in transit. In February 1941, the United Service Organization was formed. Its charter members included the following groups: the Young Men's Christian Association, the Young Women's Christian Association, the Traveler's Aid Association, the Salvation Army, the Jewish Welfare Board and the National Catholic

Rabbi Alexander Goode (second from the left) and three other chaplains surrendered their lives in a collective effort to rescue their fellow crewmen when the USAT *Dorchester* was torpedoed and sunk on the Atlantic by German U-boats. In 1944, military officials posthumously awarded the Distinguished Service Cross and Purple Heart to the four men's next of kin. The heroism of the chaplains continued to be recognized in the postwar years in extraordinary ways. In 1961, President Eisenhower bestowed a Special Medal for Heroism, a one-time award authorized by Congress on the four fallen heroes. *Image in author's possession.*

Community Service. Volunteers, mostly women, devoted countless hours to performing work at USO Center as cooks, hostesses and caseworkers. By the end of the war, some 740,000 individuals had stepped forward to volunteer for this type of volunteer war duty in more than three thousand USO Centers. Residents in the Queen City fell in line with this national trend. The city effectively mobilized volunteers to staff ten different centers. The first USO Center in the city was a modest shed built on the esplanade of Fountain Square and opened for business in May 1941. It was constructed by the labor of inmates at the city workhouse. Members of the Traveler's Aid Society operated an information center for itinerant servicemen. Three months later, officials at Union Terminal opted to convert their ground-floor restaurant, the Rookwood Tea Room (so named for its famous decorative tiles), into a USO Center.

Most visiting soldiers and sailors came to Cincinnati via troop train. For many, their first, and perhaps only, glimpse of the city came as their troop train crept through the crowded rail yard and slowed to a stop at the Union Terminal station. Many individuals opted to remain inside Union Terminal, where they could write a letter to a loved one, watch the latest newsreel at the newsreel theater just off the lobby or relax in the Tea Room. For these soldiers and sailors, their view of the Queen City was skewed. Union Terminal must have seemed like a wonderland. Union Terminal opened its doors in 1932, the worst year of the Great Depression. The developers of the new train station had taken enormous risks to construct the new facility. They went through several years of buyers' remorse because the train station was underused. By the time servicemen started arriving on troop trains in 1941, the economy had rebounded. Union Terminal was practically a city within a city. It included such amenities as a barbershop, high-end department stores and tony restaurants. As servicemen made their way up the ramps from their trains to the domed rotunda, one of the largest of its kind in the nation, they must have felt a little bit like the character Dorothy Gale in the popular film *Wizard of Oz*. The inside of the Art Deco rotunda was painted in bright yellows and oranges and featured tile mosaics that depicted the proud history of the Queen City, from its founding in 1788 up to the present.

If servicemen and women did venture beyond the Rockwood Tea Room to see what Cincinnati had to offer during their short visit, they left via the main entrance of the rotunda. Terminal officials had agreed to hang a large mural-size poster above those doors. This war production poster, approved by the OWI, showed three hands. The middle hand of a uniformed soldier grasped a rifle; it was flanked on each side by hands holding wrenches. The message that accompanied the image read: "Strong in the strength of the Lord we who fight in the people's cause will never stop until that cause is won." The message worked on a variety of levels. First, the image and text reiterated the common theme that the citizens on the home front stood united behind the soldiers on the fighting fronts. Second, it referred to America's war effort as "a people's cause," likely borrowed from British war propaganda. Churchill frequently referred to Great Britain's conflict as "a people's war." Whatever the intellectual origins of the OWI-approved poster, it served to inspire and remind those in uniform that the people of the home front supported the war and appreciated the efforts of military personnel. The OWI learned that effective propaganda required more than just a good message. Just as important was the ability to secure a good physical location so the message could be seen repeatedly and remembered. Apart from Fountain Square, the rotunda in Union Terminal probably had more foot traffic than any other part of the city. By 1944, about thirty-four thousand GIs arrived in Cincinnati each day. It has been estimated that by the end of the war some three million troops had passed through Union Terminal.

Cincinnati, like many other cities, had developed a reputation for its warm hospitality. One air cadet at Xavier University's College Training Detachment (CTD) program recalled the generosity of Cincinnatians toward people in uniform: "[Back] then it was also impossible to buy more than one drink at a bar because civilians would immediately tell the bartender to give us another drink. Sometimes several drinks would be set up at one time. After one or two drinks we would have to leave because we could not possibly accept all the drinks offered."

Typically, soldiers and sailors went to the USO Centers where they felt most welcomed. Jewish military personnel gravitated to a center on Reading Road, just north of the city. Catholic GIs often went to the Fenwick Center on East Fifth Street, operated by the Catholic archdiocese. Two clubs run by the YWCA and the YMCA on the West End offered a range of services to black members of the military in racially segregated facilities. The fact that these centers remained segregated throughout the war only gave added urgency to the "Double Victory" program that had become popular among northern blacks and many black servicemen and women. In 1943, in the large reception area of the "Negro" center on West Ninth Street, a poster hung on the wall that reminded its charges what they were fighting for:

To Our Men in the Service
As you leave Cincinnati or any other place in our United States of America
To fight to maintain Democracy (nothing but plain old everyday freedom)
The city's gratitude and prayers go with you.
We are proud of you and will support you until victory is won.
Good luck to you all the way there and back again.

The bonds between the home front and those Cincinnatians in uniform had grown strong as the war continued. Every neighborhood and community felt it had a vested interest in the safe return of its children and neighbors.

By the spring of 1944, momentum had certainly shifted toward the Allies. After dramatic victories in North Africa in 1942, Soviet forces heroically defended Stalingrad with an all-out effort and launched a successful counterattack on the Nazis in late 1943. The United States continued to push back Japanese forces in the Pacific. On May 8, 1944, General Eisenhower set the date of June 5 for the top-secret, cross-channel invasion of France known as D-day. In early June, Allied forces on the Italian Peninsula met with continued success. On June 4, British and American forces liberated Rome. Meanwhile, inclement weather forced Eisenhower to postpone the D-day invasion, code name Operation Overlord, for twenty-four hours.

After the assault was launched on June 6, President Roosevelt took to the airwaves to address the nation. Leading the nation in prayer, he warned the American people:

Their road will be long and hard. For the enemy is strong. He may hurl back our forces. Success may not come with rushing speed, but we shall return again and again; and we know that by Thy grace, and by the righteousness of our cause, our sons will triumph.

They will be sore tried, by night and by day, without rest—until the victory is won. The darkness will be rent by noise and flame. Men's souls will be shaken with the violence of war.

By the end of the day, Allied forces had secured the beaches at Normandy. British and American forces controlled a vital fifty-mile stretch of beaches on the French coastline. But Roosevelt had been correct. The military success in France came at a high cost. The combined casualties for Axis and Allied forces exceeded 110,000. The loss of American lives during the assault—more than 5,000—exceeded the number of American dead at the bloody and costly battle of Antietam during the American Civil War.

On the morning of June 6, anxious Cincinnatians gathered at Christ Church for an unplanned prayer service. Rector Nelson Burroughs estimated that a crowd of about 200 had gathered spontaneously. Bishop Hobson arrived later in the day and led the assembled masses in a noonday church service, "one of the most moving services ever held here," according to Burroughs. That evening, a group of about 450 poured into Christ Church for another service that was aired by WSAI radio. Burroughs reported that many parishioners called the next day to thank him for arranging the radio broadcast. He assured callers that the idea to air the service came from the radio station.

June 6 began as an exceptional day, according to UC president Raymond Walters. He recorded in his diary that newsboys were selling extra editions of the *Times-Star* outside his house. Later that afternoon, Walters emerged from the administration building after meeting with his board of directors for several hours. A large group had gathered on the steps outside the building for an interfaith prayer service. A rabbi read from the Old Testament and a Protestant minister and a Catholic priest each read from the New Testament. Obviously moved by the assemblage, Walters recalled: "It was a solemn night, looking down from the steps upon the faces of these youths."

On the same day, more than fifteen thousand workers left their stations at the Wright Aeronautical Corporation's assembly line. Striking workers at the aircraft engine plant walked off the job to protest the promotion of black workers, who would now work side by side with white employees. The *Cincinnati Post* lambasted the striking workers: "You Wright strikers, what will you say to the fathers and mothers of those men who fall in France?" The strike highlighted the discrepancies of a democracy waging war against fascism while it continued to treat its largest minority group as second-class citizens. After four days of work stoppage and a threat by the federal government to fire the wildcat strikers, order was finally restored at the plant. To be fair, the actions of the Wright workers represented the norm in 1940s Cincinnati as well as other midwestern industrial cities. Other war plants in the Queen City had experienced similar types of work stoppages earlier the same year. Moreover, the issues had been similar—namely, white workers flinching at the prospect of working in proximity with African Americans. What made the Wright strike "shameful," according to a *Cincinnati Post* editorialist, was the impeccably poor timing of the event.

Despite the continuing tensions in the workplace, the success on the beaches of Normandy allowed Americans on the home front, Cincinnati included, to feel hopeful about the future. By the summer of 1944, the Allies had achieved their collective goal of establishing a two-front war. This strategy, long in the planning and now finally implemented, was designed to deplete the last bits of resistance that Nazi Germany could muster. By the summer of 1944, the defeat of the Axis powers in Europe seemed a matter of "when" rather than "if."

Chapter 5

FROM VICTORY TO PEACE

A City Transformed, 1944–45

T hat the war had been an agent of change there was no doubt. Since 1941, Cincinnatians had been constantly on the move. Men and women went off to war. Those who remained behind often relocated themselves or their families to work in war plants. Despite the war-induced chaos and uncertainty, Queen City residents made an effort to maintain normal patterns of behavior. One of those patterns centered on baseball. On April 18, 1944, when the Cincinnati Reds fielded their team on Opening Day, many of the key players from the 1940 championship team were no longer on the team roster. The Reds, like every other ball club, had to scramble to find replacements for players who enlisted or were drafted. The team gambled on several older players who were past their prime, and in February, it inked a deal with a young, unproven pitcher from Hamilton, Ohio, named Joe Nuxhall. The gangly left-hander—he was only fifteen at the time—was six feet, three inches, large for his age. The Reds invited Nuxhall to sit in the dugout with the team on Opening Day, with the understanding that he would join the Reds as a player once the school year had ended. His opportunity to pitch came on June 10, 1944, just four days after the D-day invasion. The Reds went head to head with the St. Louis Cardinals. That day belonged to the Cards. By the time Nuxhall entered the game as a reliever, the Reds trailed 13–0. Nuxhall established a major-league record as the youngest person to play in a professional baseball game in the modern era. His debut with the Reds was nothing short of disastrous. The youngster contracted a sudden case of nerves. Ordinarily confident in his innate ability to throw strikes, Nuxhall could not get out of the inning. The team reassigned Nuxhall to the minors shortly after his debut. When he returned to the majors in 1952 for the Reds, he had worked out his control issues and enjoyed a long and relatively successful run with the club before becoming a local legend in the broadcast booth.

In the spring of 1944, there was a storyline bigger than baseball that rivaled the attention of most Cincinnatians. Politics was in the air. The election of 1944 yielded mixed results for Cincinnatians, who found themselves at the center of attention in three important, and somewhat interrelated, races: James Stewart's gubernatorial race, John Bricker's bid for the Republican presidential nomination and Robert Taft's reelection campaign for the U.S. Senate. For the first time in decades, Ohio's gubernatorial contest involved a Cincinnatian. In the fall of 1943, after nearly three terms as Cincinnati's mayor, James Stewart announced his intention to run for governor. Stewart won the primary election. In the general election in the fall, he squared off against Frank Lausche, the charismatic, two-term Democratic mayor of Cleveland. Lausche, it turned out, had the ability to convince a sizeable number of Republicans to vote for him. Stewart campaigned hard in the general election, but he fell short of victory.

The gubernatorial race was open to two challengers because four-term Republican governor John W. Bricker threw his hat in the ring for his party's nomination for the presidency. Robert Taft, a presidential hopeful in 1940, supported the governor's candidacy, but Bricker soon learned that he was nothing more than a favorite son of the Ohio delegates. New York governor Thomas Dewey emerged as the frontrunner and easily captured the nomination. He would oppose Franklin D. Roosevelt in his attempt to win an unprecedented fourth term in office. Bricker landed the number two spot on the ticket.

Ohioans had become accustomed to occupying the center of attention when it came to presidential elections. The state had long been regarded as one of the top electoral prizes for presidential contenders. In June, before the national political conventions transpired, *Time* magazine speculated that Ohio would once again be in the spotlight: "Politics has long traditions and high stakes in Ohio. Like Virginia, Ohio has great families and leaders who have made national politics a notable career. Like Virginia, Ohio has mothered many presidents—seven Republicans from Grant to Harding. This year Ohio's politics are once more the nation's politics."

It was a foregone conclusion that FDR would seek another term in 1944. Less clear was who would serve as the president's running mate. Many

Democratic Party leaders wanted to replace Vice President Henry Wallace, whom they viewed as too liberal. At the party's convention, delegates agreed on the nomination of Harry S. Truman, a little-known U.S. senator from Missouri, as the party's vice presidential candidate. Truman had made a name for himself in official Washington as the chair of a Senate investigation committee that exposed cases of waste and mismanagement at war plants. One of the committee's targets was the Wright Aeronautical Plant in Lockland. His committee's investigation had turned up evidence that airplane engines at the Lockland plant had not been properly inspected before being shipped out for final assembly.

Truman made several campaign appearances in Ohio during the fall election. His stump speeches worked on two levels. He acted as the proxy for FDR's reelection bid. He also made pointed speeches against Robert A. Taft's reelection. Taft often played up the fact that he spent time growing up in the White House, usually to his advantage. Truman branded Taft as the product of nepotism, plain and simple. Truman declared of his colleague, "Senator Taft is one of those unfortunate cases where the son is elected because the people remember the outstanding character of the father." Taft had bigger problems than Truman during his campaign. Organized labor, specifically the Congress of Industrial Organizations (CIO), one of the nation's most powerful labor unions, had mobilized an impressive war chest to defeat the incumbent senator. The election proved to be the toughest one in Taft's career. Many urbanites objected to Taft's conservative positions on organized labor and foreign policy. He fared better in rural counties. He prevailed on election day, winning just 50.3 percent of the popular vote. The presidential election proved to be more predictable. FDR failed to carry the Buckeye State, but his nationwide electoral victory over the Dewey-Bricker ticket proved to be decisive.

If 1944 was a year of choices, for voters, it was also a year of planning for the future. On June 22, 1944, a few weeks after the D-day invasion, Congress, with the support of both parties, passed one of the most far-reaching bills to provide for returning veterans. The Serviceman's Readjustment Act, known simply as the GI Bill of Rights, paid stipends to veterans to return to the college or university of their choosing to complete their education or to start and finish their college careers that had been interrupted by the war. The act also provided veterans with low-interest loans for mortgages or start-up costs for businesses. Locally, both Xavier University and the University of Cincinnati witnessed significant jumps in their student populations in the 1944 fall term because of the support from the federal government.

In 1944, Bishop Henry Wise Hobson (far left) departed for the western front in Europe to visit firsthand with troops in the field and the wounded in the military hospitals. *Courtesy of Christ Church Cathedral Archives.*

For the duration of the war, Cincinnatians continued to do their bit, whether as members of the armed forces or in some home front capacity. The U.S. Treasury Department continued its sponsorship of a series of war bond drives that helped pay for the war and offset inflation. Local leaders

University of Cincinnati president Raymond Walters (1932–55) guided the university through the challenges of the Great Depression and then the war years. *Courtesy of the University of Cincinnati Archives.*

in Cincinnati discovered that bond purchasers could earmark the purchase of their interest-bearing bonds for capital improvements. In 1943, members of Christ Church found a way to target war bond purchases to pay for a memorial honoring Reverend Frank Nelson, the previous rector. Likewise, in 1944, Archbishop McNicholas, with an eye on the future, encouraged pastors in charge of Catholic churches and schools to use war bonds as a form of investment. He wrote to Father Francis X. Cotter of St. Bernard in Winton Place: "I am pleased to learn that you have a few thousand dollars set aside for the extension of your school building. I hope that all in St. Bernard's will purchase a war bond, making it out in the name of your church for your school. The government drive and your own parish drive should be conducted simultaneously."

In the fall of 1944, Bishop Henry Wise Hobson announced that he would depart for the western front in France. Hobson had been an anchor of strength for the Christ Church community, helping families to deal with the war-related challenges. The Queen City's view of Hobson, the once outspoken advocate of armed intervention in Europe's war in 1940, had certainly improved by 1944. According to his colleague at Christ Church, Reverend Nelson Burroughs, Hobson was now regarded as "the Bishop of Cincinnati." Burroughs added: "You know how unpopular he was in some

Raymond Walters consistently voted against Franklin Roosevelt in every election. One day after the election of 1944, Walters tried to console himself. He confided in his diary: "I've been in the minority so much of my life, attended a college which loses so persistently at football that I have become a hard old rubber ball. I've already bounced back." *Courtesy of University of Cincinnati Archives.*

circles before we got into the war. He was straightforward and farseeing in those hard days. Now everyone respects him for the position he took, and I hope they will follow him with confidence in the future."

Letters came back to Cincinnati families from soldiers, sailors and airmen who performed their duties in far-flung locations. Sometimes they received the accolades of heroes; usually they labored without recognition of any sort. Only a small percentage engaged in combat, but many ended up serving in exotic locales far from home. Charles Stix, for example, enlisted in the marines after graduating from Walnut Hills in 1943. After a brief stint in an officer's training program, he was reassigned to basic training at Paris Island, South Carolina. By 1944, Stix was stationed in the Pacific. He saw action at Pelieu. He was involved in one of the bloodiest and lengthiest campaigns in the Pacific theater. He helped push Imperial Japanese forces off the tiny island. The Allies' strategy of securing a beachhead, then building a landing strip for planes and then moving on to the next target was called "island hopping." Each victory brought the Allies closer to the goal of a massive amphibious assault on the Japanese mainland. After Pelieu was secured, Stix was lucky enough to attend a USO show put on by fellow Ohioan Bob Hope. The talented and popular star of screen and radio took his vaudeville style of stand-up comedy to military bases across the nation and then to troops close to the front lines. Among Hollywood stars, Hope's dedicated efforts to entertain the troops were unrivalled.

Another Cincinnatian, Hilliard Dozier, a B-17 pilot stationed in Great Britain, had his own brush with a celebrity. Big bandleader and musician Glenn Miller performed with his army air corps band in a tiny village just down the road from Dozier's unit. Miller enlisted in the army air corps at the height of his popularity. After entertaining the troops, Miller departed for London for a command performance for the queen. Dozier learned that Miller had left a stack of record albums behind. Dozier flew a single-prop plane to London, attempting to return the misplaced records. When he arrived, he learned the tragic news that the bandleader, who had already departed on a plane headed for Paris, had been killed in a freak accident. Just as Miller's plane had taken off, a British bomber on its way back to its air base came into the same air space. The bomber had been unable to drop its payload of bombs on its mission target. On the return flight, the pilot of that plane followed the protocol to dump its bombs into the English Channel, striking Miller's plane in the process.

Unfortunately, some families with relatives in the service received the dreaded telegram from the War or Navy Department that began with the words "We regret to inform you..." Bernard Duwel, a first-generation German American and a successful tobacco farmer in western Hamilton County near Harrison in the 1920s, received bad news on two separate occasions. After Pearl Harbor, one of his sons, Carl, enlisted in the navy. In 1943, German U-boats torpedoed Carl's ship in the North Atlantic. The entire crew went down with the ship. Carl's younger brother, Elmer, enlisted in the army as an infantryman. When his unit saw action at the Battle of the Bulge in 1944, Elmer was killed in action. Tragedy struck twice. The Duwel family had two gold stars on display at their family homestead.

Inspired by stories like the Duwel family's, the home front carried on. More often than not, individuals took on completely new roles during

MUSIC HALL
CINCINNATI

FIFTIETH SEASON
CINCINNATI SYMPHONY ORCHESTRA

EUGENE GOOSSENS
MUSICAL DIRECTOR

THIRD PAIR SYMPHONY CONCERTS
CONDUCTED BY
EUGENE GOOSSENS

SOLOIST
JEANETTE MacDONALD
SOPRANO

THE STAR-SPANGLED BANNER

Oh say! can you see by the dawn's early light,
What so proudly we hail'd at the twilight's last gleaming,
Whose broad stripes and bright stars, thro' the perilous fight,
O'er the ramparts we watch'd were so gallantly streaming?
And the rockets red glare, the bombs bursting in air,
Gave proof thro' the night that our flag was still there.
Oh, say, does that Star-Spangled Banner yet wave
O'er the land of the free and the home of the brave?

UNITED NATIONS NATIONAL ANTHEM
No. 3, CHINA

San Min Chu I,
Our aim shall be
To free our land,
With world peace planned,
O comrades, vanguards, venture far;
Hold fast your aim by sun and star.
Be strong and brave!
Your country save!
One heart, one soul,
One mind, one goal!

SATURDAY EVENING   SUNDAY AFTERNOON
OCTOBER 28   OCTOBER 29

Left and opposite: During the 1944 CSO season, conductor Eugene Goosens continued to present inspiring and patriotic programming for his patrons. In October 1944, Jeanette MacDonald, a well-known singer and actress, made her Cincinnati debut. *Courtesy of the Cincinnati Symphony Orchestra.*

the war years. Some may have learned new skills in the process. On the other hand, a few lucky people found ways to apply their existing skill sets to benefit the war effort. Such was the case with Cincinnati Symphony conductor Eugene Goosens. While most people shelved their career aspirations for the duration of the war, Goosens somehow managed to further his professional career and support the war effort in substantive ways. As one of the country's top conductors, he continued to write ambitious and complicated works of music. At the same time, he delighted his regular CSO audiences with weekly tributes to men in the armed forces and the various Allied nations.

A select few Cincinnatians contributed to the war effort in a new way in the fall of 1944. Powell Crosley Jr. had been working with the Roosevelt administration since the early days of the war to assemble a shortwave transmitting station powerful enough to send propaganda messages from the Office of War Information into Axis-occupied territories. The federal government took over a 640-acre chunk of farmland in West Chester about thirty miles north of Cincinnati in southeastern Butler County. Officials agreed on the location because it was inland enough to be secure from possible enemy attacks, and in 1942, it had access to adequate power grids. By the fall of 1944, OWI's Voice of America (VOA) programming had begun from the Bethany Station in West Chester. For years, Germany had dominated the radio airwaves with its propaganda aimed at its civilian population as well as Allied prisoners of war. For the duration of the war, VOA programs reached their intended audiences. Infuriated about this new development, Hitler referred to the people who created VOA programs as "the Cincinnati liars."

As the United States entered its fourth year of hostilities, the Queen City found itself on the receiving end of recognitions from branches of the armed forces. Cincinnati was twice honored by the U.S. Merchant Marines with transport ships that bore names of well-known individuals or institutions. On December 6, 1944, a day before the third anniversary of the attack on Pearl Harbor, Rabbi Jonah B. Wise of New York helped christen the *Isaac Mayer Wise*, a troop transport ship named after his father, the founder of Reform Judaism in North America and the founder of Hebrew Union College. The launching of the Liberty ship took place at the St. John's Shipbuilding Corporation in Jacksonville, Florida. These prefabricated ships, constructed rapidly, transported vital materials—including fuel, food and ammunition—to the fighting fronts. At the launching ceremony, Rabbi Wise drew on the connection of his father's life work and the current struggle being waged against fascism: "Isaac M. Wise sought not only liberty for himself in this land, but he helped to create

On March 7, 1945, navy lieutenant Dan Heekin (above, left), an Xavier University alumnus, helped Mrs. Edelie Carpenter, the wife of a shipyard worker, christen the SS *Xavier Victory* in Richmond, California. *Courtesy of Xavier University Archives.*

liberty and freedom for the Jews from their European shackles. It is fitting and proper, therefore, that the liberties he helped create should be carried back from these shores to Europe, as they will be by this good ship and its gallant crew."

In January 1945, the U.S. Maritime Commission bestowed a similar honor on the Xavier University community. XU was one of a handful of colleges and universities in the nation to have victory ships named after their institutions. At the March 7, 1945 christening ceremony at the massive Henry J. Kaisar Shipyards in Richmond, California, navy lieutenant Dan Heeking, an Xavier alum, paid tribute to his school. The ship, he suggested, represented a fitting way to honor the forty-three Xavier men "who have given their lives on all battlefronts, on the seas, and in aerial warfare, since December 7, 1941." He ended his remarks with a wish for the ship and its crew: "May the *S.S. Xavier Victory* sail safely and triumphantly as a unit of the greatest fleet in the world and may the men of her crew know the same spirit which inspires the men of Xavier whose motto is 'All for One and One for All.'"

As the Allied armies eked out hard-won victories in Europe and the Pacific, the leaders of the Grand Alliance met to map out a shared vision for the world after the fighting stopped. In February 1945, Roosevelt and Churchill traveled great distances and at considerable risk to meet with Soviet premier Joseph Stalin at a town in the Crimean Peninsula called Yalta. For seven days, the Allied leaders conferred on such weighty topics as the postwar partition of Germany, the creation of a free and independent Polish nation, Soviet participation in the Pacific theater and the form and function of a postwar union of nations that would promote and sustain world peace.

When Roosevelt returned to the United States, he addressed a joint session of Congress. Since his days on the campaign trail in 1932, FDR had prided himself on his indefatigable strength and tenacity. Even though his bout with polio in the 1920s left him paralyzed from the waist down, Roosevelt prided himself on his ability to deliver lengthy addresses while standing at lecterns or podiums. Throughout much of his presidency, many Americans overlooked his physical impairment. Many editorial cartoons, in fact, depicted FDR as able bodied. By February 1944, Roosevelt's health, which had long been a concern of his doctors, had further deteriorated.

When he addressed Congress, he did so from a seated position. He even made a crude if oblique reference to the "ten pounds of steel" (his leg braces) that he lugged around each day. What seems obvious in retrospect—

FDR was declining in health, to the point of incapacity or death—was unthinkable to a generation that had partnered with this wartime leader. Roosevelt left Washington, D.C., in April to regain his strength at the "Little White House" in Warm Springs, Georgia. On April 12, 1945, Roosevelt suffered a massive cerebral hemorrhage from which he never recovered. News of the president's death traveled swiftly across the nation and around the world. David Brinkley, then a young reporter in wartime Washington, D.C., recalled reading the news flash from the wire service. It was the shortest message he had ever read—"FDR Dead."

In mostly conservative, Republican Cincinnati, the news of FDR's death yielded a range of reactions and emotions. Jane Webb, a nineteen-year-old, who had grown up in a staunch Republican family of Hoover supporters, recalled, "Roosevelt was like a monarch. He became President when I was in first grade. His dynasty continued through my entire grade and high school career and into my first year of college—Imagine!"

Despite her pro-Republican attitude, Webb asked the question that countless supporters of the president asked of themselves or others: "Could we possibly manage without him?" Robert Bales, a fifteen-year-old high school dropout, had just returned from working his shift at the Wright Aeronautical Plant. Bales recalled: "FDR's death came as a shock to all of us, young and old. The President had been elected to a fourth term for the purpose of ending our hostilities…now he is dead. What are we to do? He was our commander in chief. He knew all of what was going on and our military was making great gains on all fronts. Very little…was known of V[ice] P[resident] Harry S. Truman at the time."

First Lady Eleanor Roosevelt traveled to Warm Springs by train and made arrangements for her husband's funeral. The late president's train traveled to the nation's capital, where he would lie in state at the Capitol for several days. Raymond Walters learned about the president's death when he was boarding a train bound for Washington, D.C. He and UC vice-president Norman Auburn went there to lobby naval officials to award UC a Naval Reserve Officers Training Corps program. Walters arrived in Washington on April 13 and described the mood of the nation's capital:

> *Upon the Capitol against a lovely April-blue sky the national colors hung at half-mast today, as they did on a host of buildings throughout the land. Americans mourn the passing of their President. Agree or disagree with Franklin Roosevelt (in recent years I have largely disagreed), he was a figure of such power and vitality as to merit the designation: a great American.*

When he returned home the following day, Walters delivered a midafternoon speech memorializing Roosevelt at the Hotel Gibson. After his remarks, he joined "the throng in Walnut Hills and Fountain Square in standing silently from 3 to 3:01, as the Washington service began." All over the city, people paused to mourn the passing of the leader who had guided them through the challenges of the Depression years and almost to a victorious conclusion of the current war. Flags fluttered at half-mast at Union Terminal and around the city. Walters noted that "university classes were omitted this morning; the city offices and many others were closed."

Less than a month later, on May 8, 1945, President Truman informed the nation that the war in Europe was over. Flags were still flying at half-mast to honor FDR. Russian, British and American troops converged on Berlin. The Nazis capitulated. Hitler avoided capture and the facing of a war crimes trial by committing suicide in his Berlin bunker. Boisterous and jubilant crowds gathered spontaneously at Fountain Square to celebrate the news of the victory. Hitler was hanged in effigy. No one seemed to object. A hastily mounted sign in a nearby storefront window read: "Victory is Ours. The super race has fallen. Let's finish off the Japs." That morning, the *Cincinnati Enquirer* ran a front-page story with a headline previewing the president's remarks. The paper also reminded revelers of the obvious—the war was only half over. Just under the headline, the editors included a large cartoon of Uncle Sam, decked out in combat fatigues and helmet. He held a machine gun in one hand and held the other hand up high in a dramatic "stop" gesture. The accompanying caption read, "Hold it! This war isn't over. Don't make V-Day a Spree Day!" The message was clear. The time for lengthy celebrations had not yet arrived. Parties and shopping sprees would have to wait. As long as American troops in the Pacific remained in harm's way, those on the home front understood that vital work still needed to be done.

When Harry Truman assumed the powers of the presidency in April 1945, he had no working knowledge of Allied war strategies in Europe or the Pacific or of the Manhattan Project, his own country's efforts to manufacture an atomic bomb. Replacing a popular wartime president, Truman had to quickly earn the trust of his generals and advisors *and* the American people. In late July, while meeting with Stalin and Clement Atlee, the recently elected prime minister of Great Britain, at the Potsdam Conference, Truman received word from test facilities in New Mexico that the United States had successfully detonated its first atomic bomb. Without hesitation, the president authorized the deployment of atomic bombs to end the war against Japan.

On August 6, 1945, army air corps colonel Paul W. Tibbetts piloted a B-29 Super Fortress from the tiny Pacific island Tinian in the Northern Marianas. Before entering the military, Tibbetts had completed part of his undergraduate studies at the University of Cincinnati in the 1930s. An experienced pilot of larger aircraft who had completed numerous combat missions over Europe, Tibbetts had been training for this mission since 1944. His plane, the *Enola Gay*, named after his Illinois mother, lifted off on that August morning with a payload containing a uranium-enriched atomic bomb, known to those who made it as "Little Boy." His crew dropped the bomb on the Japanese city of Hiroshima, wreaking total devastation on the city and many of its inhabitants. Three days later, a second American crew dropped an even more destructive atomic bomb on the Japanese city of Nagasaki.

News of the bombs generated excitement and anticipation that the war would soon be over. Details about the massive casualties were not known at the time. A debate over the moral implications of the use of atomic weapons would eventually transpire. But in August 1945, Americans expressed relief and gratitude. On August 10, Xavier president Celestine Steiner offered these insights to the *Cincinnati Enquirer*: "We thank God that our nation has had the will and the strength to see this great war against brutality and aggression through to final victory."

On August 15, Imperial Japan officially surrendered, and World War II was finally over. News of the impending surrender had been reported most of the day on August 14. Raymond Walters recorded the happy memory in his diary that evening:

> *Precisely one hour ago the world heard the glad news. President Truman announced to the newspaper and radio men at the White House that Emperor Hirohito accepted for his Empire of Japan the surrender terms set by the Allies. Listening to station WLW, Bob O Link* [his pet name for his wife] *and I received the word quietly in our sitting room. I kissed her. There was happiness ineffable in our hearts as we thought of our three sons in the Armed Forces.*

On August 15, a two-day celebration unfolded in the Queen City. Cincinnatians had been mentally and psychologically preparing for this day. On Fountain Square, a civil defense siren blared. At one point, the large crowd helped open up a huge American flag, said to be the third largest in the country. The mood was festive and the celebration went on for hours.

CHRIST CHURCH
CINCINNATI

A Service of Thanksgiving for Victory
V-J DAY - - 1945

✠

HYMN 430

God of our fathers, whose almighty hand
Leads forth in beauty all the starry band
Of shining worlds in splendor through the skies,
Our grateful songs before thy throne arise.

Thy love divine hath led us in the past,
In this free land by thee our lot is cast;
Be thou our ruler, guardian, guide, and stay,
Thy word our law, thy paths our chosen way.

From war's alarms, from deadly pestilence,
Be thy strong arm our ever sure defense;
Thy true religion in our hearts increase,
Thy bounteous goodness nourish us in peace.

Refresh thy people on their toilsome way,
Lead us from night to never-ending day;
Fill all our lives with love and grace divine,
And glory, laud, and praise be ever thine.   Amen.

Minister: Thine, O Lord, is the greatness, and the power, and the glory, and
the victory, and the majesty; for all that is in the heavens and in the earth is
thine; thine is the kingdom, O Lord, and thou art exalted as head above all.
   Thanks be to God, which giveth us the victory, through our Lord Jesus
Christ.

HYMN 173

The strife is o'er, the battle done,
The victory of life is won;
The song of triumph has begun.
                    Alleluia!

The powers of death have done their worst,
But Christ their legions hath dispersed:
Let shout of holy joy outburst.
                    Alleluia!

Lord by the stripes which wounded thee,
From death's dread sting thy servants free,
That we may live and sing to thee.
                    Alleluia!   Amen.

STATEMENT OF OUR PURPOSE *(The congregation seated)*

HYMN 249

All people that on earth do dwell,
Sing to the Lord with cheerful voice:
Him serve with fear, his praise forth tell,
Come ye before him and rejoice.

Praise God, from whom all blessings flow!
Praise him, all creatures here below!
Praise him above, ye heavenly host!
Praise Father, Son, and Holy Ghost!   Amen.

Christ Church was among several churches to hold special religious services
just after V-J Day. *Courtesy of Christ Church Cathedral Archives.*

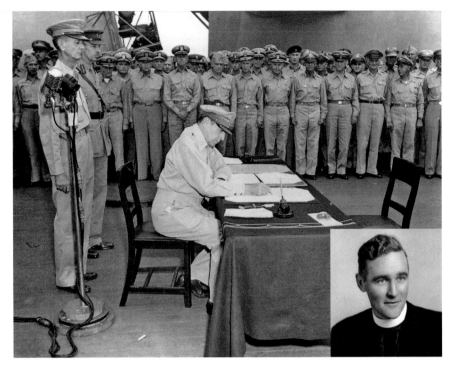

Future Cincinnatian and Xavier University president Father Paul O'Connor (inset), a Jesuit priest and navy chaplain, was assigned to the USS *Missouri*. On September 2, 1945, O'Connor stood at attention on a deck just above General Douglas MacArthur and watched him accept the formal terms of surrender from Imperial Japan. *Courtesy of Xavier University Archives.*

That evening, many area churches and synagogues held impromptu worship services. Catholics at St. Aloysius in Bridgetown "sang a hearty" *Te Deum*, an ancient fourth-century prayer of thanksgiving.

As the world made the transition from six long years of chaos and turmoil to a new postwar period of peace, Cincinnatians found themselves at the center of many important events. That fall, an appropriate coda occurred in the professional career of CSO conductor Eugene Goosens. After years of arranging concerts that paid tribute to the various countries that had sworn to defeat the Axis powers, Goosens received the special honor of being named guest conductor of the San Francisco Symphony Orchestra for the United Nations Conference held in that city. After the delegates of the forty-four nations signed the UN charter in October 1945, the new organization had to decide where its global headquarters would be located. Cincinnati mayor James Stewart traveled to London with a delegation of city officials to lobby the merits of the Queen City for this honor. The subcommittee obviously ruled against Stewart, citing the city's inland location and its isolationist views.

In 1955, Hamilton County opened a new downtown branch for its public library. Ten years after the cessation of hostilities, city officials dedicated the new facility to the men and women who served in the armed forces during World War II. By that time, as was characteristic of that generation, most of those people who had given so much of themselves during the war years—whether serving in uniform or in some home front capacity—had quietly moved on with their lives. Lieutenants became accountants. WACs traded in their khakis for aprons. Air raid wardens went back to working as funeral directors. After eleven years of economic hardships during the Great Depression, followed by all the uncertainties of the war years, Cincinnatians eagerly embraced and welcomed the new challenges and opportunities of the postwar era.

SUGGESTIONS FOR FURTHER READING

"Cincinnati Goes to War." *Queen City Heritage* (Spring 1991): 21–80.

Federal Writers Project of the WPA. *They Built a City: 150 Years of Industrial Cincinnati*. Cincinnati, OH, 1938.

Fortin, Roger. *To See Great Wonders: A History of Xavier University, 1831–2006*. Scranton, PA: Scranton University Press, 2006.

Hoard, Greg. *Joe: Rounding Third and Heading for Home*. Wilmington, OH: Orange Frazier Press, 2004.

Lindenmeyer, Kriste. "Views from the Life of Paul Briol: Cincinnati's Unconventional Photographer." *Queen City Heritage* (Fall 1989): 9–24.

McGrane, Reginald. *The University of Cincinnati: A Success Story in Urban Higher Education*. New York: Harper and Row, 1963.

Miller, Robert Earnest. "April 12, 1945—The Other 'Day of Infamy': Remembering and Commemorating the Death of FDR." In Andrew E. Kersten and Kriste Lindenmeyer, eds., *Politics and Progress: Defining the State and Society in America since 1865*. Westport, CT: Greenwood Press, 2001.

———. *Cincinnati: The World War II Years*. Charleston, SC: Arcadia Publishing, 2004.

———. "The War That Never Came: Civilian Defense in Cincinnati, Ohio during World War II." *Queen City Heritage* (Spring 1992): 2–22.

Morris, J. Wesley. *Christ Church: 1817–1967*. Cincinnati, OH: Episcopal Church of Cincinnati, 1967.

Patterson, James T. *Mr. Republican: A Biography of Robert A. Taft*. Boston: Houghton Mifflin, 1972.

Rhodes, Greg, and John Snyder. *Redleg Journal: Year by Year and Day by Day with the Cincinnati Reds Since 1866.* Cincinnati, OH: Road West Publishing, 2000.

Thierstein, Eldred A. *Cincinnati Opera: From the Zoo to Music Hall.* Cincinnati, OH: Deerstone Books, 1995.

Winkler, Alan M. "The Queen City and World War II." *Queen City Heritage* (Spring 1991): 3–20.

WPA Guide to Cincinnati. Cincinnati Historical Society, 1987. Reprint of 1943 edition.

INDEX

ABOUT THE AUTHOR

Robert Earnest (Bob) Miller is a native of the Cincinnati area, having grown up in Bridgetown. He currently resides in Warren County, Ohio. Miller earned his PhD in history from the University of Cincinnati. He teaches history at the University of Cincinnati–Clermont College. Miller is the author of *Cincinnati: The War Years* (2004) and *Hamilton County Parks* (2006). He has worked on several public history projects at the local, state and national levels, including the award-winning World War II exhibit entitled "Cincinnati Goes to War: A Community Responds to Total War" for the Cincinnati Museum Center.

Visit us at
www.historypress.net

....

This title is also available as an e-book